Frommer's®

Athens
day BY day™

1st Edition

by Tania Kollias

WILEY
Wiley Publishing, Inc.

Contents

Wiley Publishing, Inc.

111 River St.
Hoboken, NJ 07030-5774

ISBN 978-0-470-28567-1

Editor: Emil J. Ross
Production Editor: Jana M. Stefanciosa
Photo Editor: Richard Fox with Photo Affairs
Cartographer: Andrew Dolan
Production by Wiley Indianapolis Composition Services

For information on our other products and services or to obtain technical support, please contact our Customer Care Department within the U.S. at 800/762-2974, outside the U.S. at 317/572-3993 or fax 317/572-4002.

Wiley also publishes its books in a variety of electronic formats. Some content that appears in print may not be available in electronic formats.

Manufactured in China

5   4   3   2   1

A Note from the Publisher

Organizing your time. That's what this guide is all about.

Other guides give you long lists of things to see and do and then expect you to fit the pieces together. The Day by Day guides are different. These guides tell you the best of everything, and then they show you how to see it *in the smartest, most time-efficient way.* Our authors have designed detailed itineraries organized by time, neighborhood, or special interest. And each tour comes with a bulleted map that takes you from stop to stop.

Hoping to see the best museums in Athens or stroll around the Acropolis? Planning a walk through Syntagma Square, or plotting a day in the Greek islands? Whatever your interest or schedule, the Day by Days give you the smartest routes to follow. Not only do we take you to the top attractions, hotels, and restaurants, but we also help you access those special moments that locals get to experience—those "finds" that turn tourists into travelers.

The Day by Days are also your top choice if you're looking for one complete guide for all your travel needs. The best hotels and restaurants for every budget, the greatest shopping values, the wildest nightlife—it's all here.

Why should you trust our judgment? Because our authors personally visit each place they write about. They're an independent lot who say what they think and would never include places they wouldn't recommend to their best friends. They're also open to suggestions from readers. If you'd like to contact them, please send your comments my way at mspring@wiley.com, and I'll pass them on.

Enjoy your Day by Day guide—the most helpful travel companion you can buy. And have the trip of a lifetime.

Warm regards,

Michael Spring

Michael Spring
Publisher
Frommer's Travel Guides

About the Author

Tania Kollias grew up in Vancouver, Canada, and graduated from Simon Fraser University. She has traveled through southeast Asia and Europe, lived in Australia and Japan, and now resides in Athens, Greece, where she works as a journalist, writer, and editor. She covers Greece for *Frommer's Europe by Rail* and *Europe For Dummies*.

An Additional Note

Please be advised that travel information is subject to change at any time—and this is especially true of prices. We therefore suggest that you write or call ahead for confirmation when making your travel plans. The authors, editors, and publisher cannot be held responsible for the experiences of readers while traveling. Your safety is important to us, however, so we encourage you to stay alert and be aware of your surroundings.

Star Ratings, Icons & Abbreviations

Every hotel, restaurant, and attraction listing in this guide has been ranked for quality, value, service, amenities, and special features using a **star-rating system.** Hotels, restaurants, attractions, shopping, and nightlife are rated on a scale of zero stars (recommended) to three stars (exceptional). In addition to the star-rating system, we also use a **kids** icon to point out the best bets for families. Within each tour, we recommend cafes, bars, or restaurants where you can take a break. Each of these stops appears in a shaded box marked with a coffee-cup-shaped bullet ☕ .

The following **abbreviations** are used for credit cards:

AE	American Express	DISC	Discover	V	Visa
DC	Diners Club	MC	MasterCard		

Frommers.com

Now that you have this guidebook to help you plan a great trip, visit our web-site at **www.frommers.com** for additional travel information on more than 4,000 destinations. We update features regularly to give you instant access to the most current trip-planning information available. At Frommers.com, you'll find scoops on the best airfares, lodging rates, and car rental bargains. You can even book your travel online through our reliable travel booking partners. Other popular features include:

- Online updates of our most popular guidebooks
- Vacation sweepstakes and contest giveaways
- Newsletters highlighting the hottest travel trends
- Podcasts, interactive maps, and up-to-the-minute events listings
- Opinionated blog entries by Arthur Frommer himself
- Online travel message boards with featured travel discussions

A Note on Prices

In the "Take a Break" and "Best Bets" sections of this book, we have used a system of dollar signs to show a range of costs for 1 night in a hotel (the price of a double-occupancy room) or the cost of an entree at a restaurant. Use the following table to decipher the dollar signs:

Cost	Hotels	Restaurants
$	under $100	under $10
$$	$100–$200	$10–$20
$$$	$200–$300	$20–$30
$$$$	$300–$400	$30–$40
$$$$$	over $400	over $40

An Invitation to the Reader

In researching this book, we discovered many wonderful places—hotels, restaurants, shops, and more. We're sure you'll find others. Please tell us about them, so we can share the information with your fellow travelers in upcoming editions. If you were disappointed with a recommendation, we'd love to know that, too. Please write to:

Frommer's Athens Day by Day, 1st Edition
Wiley Publishing, Inc. • 111 River St. • Hoboken, NJ 07030-5774

16 Favorite
Moments

16 Favorite Moments

16 Favorite **Moments**

1. Gaze at the Acropolis
2. Sip coffee at Thissio Square
3. Celebrate Kathara Deftera
4. Look out from Pnyx
5. Psyrri by night
6. Find a cultural gem
7. Experience an outdoor theater
8. Walk the Grand Promenade
9. Wander the "handyman" alleys off Athinas Street
10. Shop for shoes on Ermou
11. Admire Adrianou's souvies
12. Eat a souvlaki on "Kebab Street"
13. Sail from Piraeus
14. Barter at the Gazi flea market
15. Take in Monastiraki's Adrianou Street
16. Browse the neighborhood farmer's market

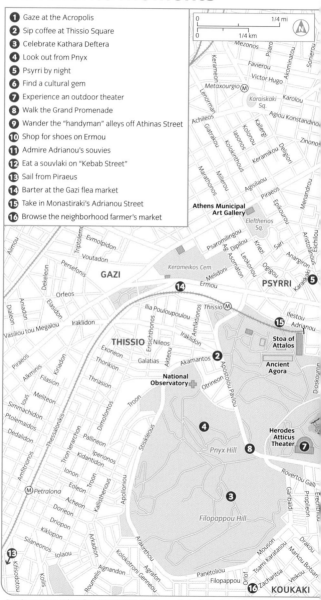

Previous page: When floodlit at night, the Acropolis is visible from almost every corner of Athens.

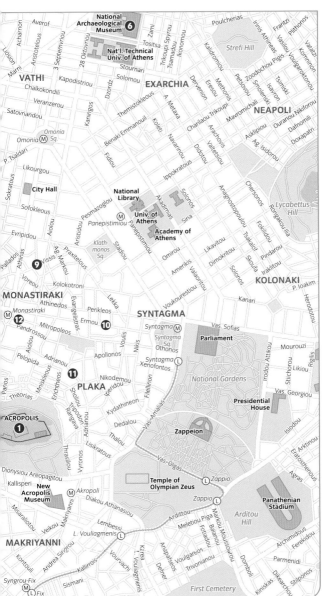

Athens may have the Parthenon, that most exquisite symbol of achievement, but this free, anarchic city is more than just a monumental collection of 5th-century-B.C. landmarks. Beside the ancient sites in the compact, historic center lie pedestrian walkways lined with modern bars, cafes, and tavernas, where the food is piled high, the barrel wine flows freely, and the patrons are animated. Kicking dance clubs and luxurious post-Olympic hotels down scenic streets are only a short walk away. And then there's the shopping, from the latest shoes to classical craftsmanship. What follows is a collection of some of the best of these diversions, both antique and contemporary.

1 Gaze at the Acropolis. There is no comparison anywhere to the wonder that is the Acropolis. The Parthenon-topped apex has been Greece's pride and joy since antiquity—and ancient Greeks were as distracted by its beauty as we are. Eyes are drawn to it, streets lead to it, and thankfully, given its location, it's not too hard to get a view of it. It's absolutely spectacular at night. *See p 9.*

2 Sip coffee at Thissio Square. Sitting here with friends or family at an outdoor cafe is relaxing, especially for parents. (Kids can play without fear of traffic.) This is

Athinaion Politeia, a cafe in Thissio Square, a stone's throw from the Ancient Agora and Acropolis.

A girl flying a kite on Pnyx Hill for Clean Monday, the beginning of Greek Orthodox Great Lent.

where you get that million-dollar view of both the aforementioned Acropolis and Lycabettus Hill. *See p 9.*

3 Celebrate Kathara Deftera. A couple of months after Christmas, children start appearing in costumes for Carnival. Then Kathara Deftera, the first day of Lent, is upon us, and families gather on **Filopappou Hill,** or any other windy spot, for the traditional flying of kites. If there's a breeze, expect to see thousands. *See p 31.*

④ Look out from Pnyx. On this "thank God" hill in the middle of town, you will see a lot of people from neighboring areas bringing their apartment-balcony-confined dogs here to, well, poop. But many others, like me, come up to see the celebrated Attic sky (Greece's light is known for its clarity), look out to sea, and watch the sunset from a natural setting. *See p 83.*

⑤ Psyrri by night. Quality of life in Athens is directly related to the fact that you can go out on foot at any hour and not worry about personal safety. The Psyrri district is full of bars, clubs, and restaurants, and the atmosphere rightly feels like a carnival. This is life as it should be. *See p 13.*

⑥ Find a cultural gem. There are so many museums and galleries in Athens, top-notch or not, that you could see something new and interesting every Sunday afternoon. State museums are also free in winter—a great public gesture. Finding one in a charming neighborhood followed by a coffee makes for a red-letter day. *See p 24.*

⑦ Experience an outdoor theater. You could visit a neighborhood

Cyclists biking the Grand Promenade, which follows Dionysiou Areopagitou and Apostolou Pavlou streets around the Acropolis.

open-air cinema to see a first-run movie, complete with a glass of wine at intermission, in a breezy garden on a warm evening. For live action, head to the Athens Epidaurus Festival in summer for an **ancient theater** performance of *Carmen,* for example. *See p 122.*

⑧ Walk the Grand Promenade. The name is used only for ease of reference for tourists, but walking along this pedestrian walkway around the Acropolis, with its breathtaking view, and stopping at a cafe for a frappe, is still way up there, even for natives. *See p 9.*

Dining under the Acropolis in the Plaka district, the area around Kydathineon and Adrianou streets.

The port city of Piraeus has been inhabited since the 26th century B.C.

⑨ Wander the "handyman" alleys off Athinas Street. Athens is hearteningly full of independent businesses, with many conveniently grouped by what they sell. (Looking for bath- and kitchenware? Go to Vissis St.) Many of these shop-filled lanes lie off Athinas Street, a main artery. *See p 65.*

⑩ Shop for shoes on Ermou. There are so many shoe stores on the pedestrian **Ermou Street** that finding the perfect pair of boots is practically a sport. Comparison window-shop for good-quality leather shoes at great prices before choosing. *See p 59.*

⑪ Admire Adrianou's souvies. Some souvenirs on heavily touristed **Adrianou Street** in Plaka seem to get better each season, while others there remain tacky. (Apparently, the biggest sellers these days are fridge magnets.) *See p 63.*

⑫ Eat a souvlaki on "Kebab Street." The bottom of **Mitropoleos Street,** at the Monastiraki Metro station, is closed off with tables from grill tavernas, so you can sit down in the middle of your shopping and have a full souvlaki meal, or a couple of skewers and a beer. How great is that? *See p 99.*

⑬ Sail from Piraeus. This neighboring city may be hectic and dirty, but its port, the busiest in Europe, is extremely practical, particularly since you can walk from the Athens Metro station, jump on a ferry at the last minute, and soon be on an island far from the bustle of the city. And I love watching the boats, especially as they dock. *See p 87.*

⑭ Barter at the Gazi flea market. The Monastiraki flea market has some good finds, but this Sunday one, opposite the cemetery of Kerameikos, has the real junk. *See p 79.*

⑮ Take in Monastiraki's Adrianou Street. There are two Adrianou Streets, and this one is great for sitting at an outdoor cafe in summer or winter (under heaters) and people-watching. A view of the Acropolis and Hephaisteion temple across the Metro line in the Ancient Agora doesn't hurt. *See p 63.*

⑯ Browse the neighborhood farmer's market. Known as *laiki,* these markets set up once a week all over Athens—each neighborhood on a different day. You can buy fresh fruits and veggies, fish, kitchenware, flowers—my favorite, and often the only thing I buy—and even carpets. My local, the Koukaki market, is on Fridays. *See p 19.* ●

The Best **in One Day**

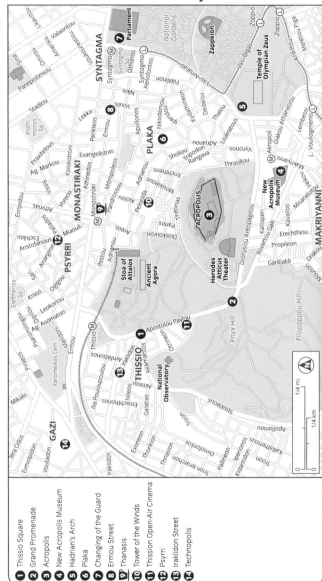

1 Thissio Square
2 Grand Promenade
3 Acropolis
4 New Acropolis Museum
5 Hadrian's Arch
6 Plaka
7 Changing of the Guard
8 Ermou Street
9 Thanasis
10 Tower of the Winds
11 Thission Open-Air Cinema
12 Psyrri
13 Iraklidon Street
14 Technopolis

Previous Page: A statue of a discus thrower, a take on the classic Greek Discobolus of Myron bronze, watches over Panathenian Stadium.

If you've only got one day in town, get a good night's sleep, because you can see most of the big sights, enjoy the shopping, and sample the foods of Athens in one fell swoop—if you work for it. The historic center—encompassing the neighborhoods of Monastiraki, Plaka, Syntagma, Psyrri, and Thissio—is quite compact and easy to orient yourself by, as the Acropolis is visible from just about anywhere. Just remember to put your walking shoes on, pack a camera, and fill your water bottle. START: **Metro to Thissio.**

1 ★★★ Thissio Square. It's a special occasion, so stop at this convenient-to-the-Metro square for your (rather pricey) morning coffee or cafe-frappe and a toast (which in Greece means a grilled cheese or grilled ham-and-cheese sandwich). Go for a table (try **Athinaion Politeia,** 33 Apostolou Pavlou and 1 Akamantos sts.; ☎ 210/341-3795) far into the square toward the Ancient Agora at the back (east) and soak up the sight of both the Acropolis and Lycabettus Hill. The view is also magical at night, when both edifices are lit up. *Apostolou Pavlon & Iraklidon sts.*

2 ★★★ Grand Promenade. Nobody calls it that, but the stroll along the cobblestone walkway that connects the ancient sites and monuments in the historic center is truly grand—especially the stroll around the Acropolis—and a popular lovers' lane in the evening, when couples straddle its low walls. Meander past or even through ancient pine, olive, and cypress groves and enjoy the views of the Acropolis, Lycabettus Hill, the Observatory on Pnyx Hill, and the Filopappou Monument atop Filopappou Hill on your way to the Acropolis. *Apostolou Pavlou/Dionysiou Areopagitou sts.*

3 ★★★ kids Acropolis. The 2,400-year-old temple to the city's patron saint, Athena, is an architectural masterpiece and a beloved symbol of Greece. It was intact until 1687, when the Venetians tried to dislodge the long-ruling Turks. A major controversy revolves around the marble statues that originally decorated the Parthenon and other buildings on the Acropolis: At the nadir of the scramble to amass antiquities while Greece was under occupation in the early 19th century, Britain's Lord Elgin chiseled off these friezes, which are now displayed in the British Museum—though Greece claims they rightfully belong in Athens. Greece has built a new museum to house them upon their longed-for, and many believe inevitable, return.

Four Caryatids ("maiden" columns) supporting a porch on the Erechtheion.

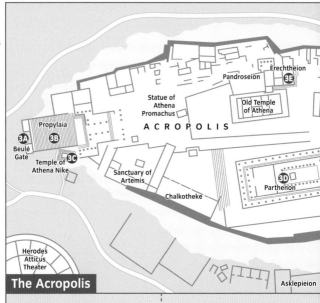

The Acropolis

The Parthenon—the all-marble temple of Athena Parthenos ("Athena the Virgin") atop the Sacred Rock of the Acropolis—was built to mathematical precision between 447 and 438 B.C., marking an apex in Doric architecture. The architects, Ictinus and Callicrates, made curved surfaces appear level, bulging columns appear straight, and inclined columns appear parallel. Once housing a 12m (40-ft.) gold-and-ivory statue by Pheidias (a small Roman copy is in the National Archaeological Museum), it has been used as Orthodox and Catholic churches, a mosque, and a munitions storehouse, which was its undoing after 2,000 years. It is now undergoing its most extensive restoration to date. After the ticket entrance, you first pass through the **3A Beulé Gate**—built by the Romans in A.D. 267 but known by the name of the French archaeologist who discovered it in 1852. Beyond lies the **3B Propylaia,** the monumental 5th-century-B.C.

entranceway. The little **3C Temple of Athena Nike** ("Athena Victory"), a beautifully proportioned Ionic temple built in 424 B.C. where citizens prayed for success, is perched above the Propylaia. It was restored in the 1930s and is being rebuilt once more. Off to the left of the **3D Parthenon,** the temple of Athena the Virgin, is the **3E Erechtheion,** which the Athenians honored as the tomb of Erechtheus, a legendary king. ⏱ *1 hr. Dionysiou Areopagitou St.* ☎ *210/321-0219. www.culture.gr. Coupon booklet 12€ adults (many categories, including archaeology students, are admitted free; ask or check website for free-admission days) valid for 4 days; includes the Acropolis, Ancient Agora, Theater of Dionysus, south slope, Kerameikos cemetery, Roman Forum, north slope & the Temple of Olympian Zeus. Daily 8am–7pm; reduced winter hours. Metro: Akropoli or bus: 230.*

④ ★★ kids New Acropolis Museum. The brand-new museum (expected to open in 2009) faces the Acropolis on Dionysiou Areopagitou Street. Some 300 marble statues weighing up to 2.5 tons each were moved off the hill for the first time in 2006 and 2007. Four of the original Caryatids, sculpted women taking the place of columns or architectural supports, from the Erechtheion (see p 10) have been moved here (one had disappeared during Ottoman rule; another is in the British Museum), together with the entire collection from the old museum, including sculptures from the Parthenon burnt by the Persians, statues of *korai* (maidens) dedicated to Athena, figures of *kouri* (young men), and many other finds from the Acropolis, comprising some 4,000 works altogether—ten times the number previously on display. An area is set aside in anticipation of the return of the Elgin marbles (see p 27). ⏱ *1–2 hr. 2–4 Makriyanni St.* ☎ *210/924-1043 (info only). www.newacropolis museum.gr. Metro: Akropoli.*

⑤ Hadrian's Arch. Facing Plaka and the Acropolis is Hadrian's triumphal arch, on a main Athens thoroughfare (Amalias Ave.). This gate from the "old" city of Athens to the "new" Roman one is made of Pentelic (from nearby Mt. Pendeli)

A whitewashed winding backstreet in Plaka, the oldest district of Athens.

marble and Corinthian-capital-topped columns, built in A.D. 131–132 in honor of Emperor Hadrian. It bears two inscriptions: facing west (toward the old town), THIS IS ATHENS, ONCE THE CITY OF THESEUS, and facing east (toward the new town), Hadrian's rebuke, THIS IS NOT THESEUS'S CITY. *Amalias Ave. & Dionysiou Areopagitou St.*

⑥ ★★★ kids Plaka. Stop for lunch or an early dinner in this pedestrian zone; the food is nothing special, but the atmosphere makes up for it. Do some souvenir shopping, too, especially along Adrianou (Hadrian's) and Pandrossou streets, before or after wandering through

The entrance to the New Acropolis Museum overlooks the Makriyanni excavation site.

any number of the island-village-like alleys. *Adrianou & Kydathineon sts.*

7 ★★ kids **Changing of the Guard.** The Presidential Guard keeps watch over the Tomb of the Unknown Soldier, and two soldiers engage in elaborate ceremonial exercises on the hour. See p 33, **2**.

8 ★★★ **Ermou Street.** You can't leave Greece without buying a pair of stylish leather shoes, or at least the iconic sandals. Pedestrianized Ermou (Hermes) Street has always been one of Athens's busiest, and all the main chain stores are here, alongside Greek shoemakers. The street goes from Parliament all the way down (west) past the Monastiraki and Thissio Metro stations to the ancient Kerameikos cemetery and old gasworks-turned-cultural-center Technopolis in Gazi. *Ermou & Athinas sts.*

9 **Thanasis.** One of 3 or 4 *mageiria* ("cookhouses") at the end of the pedestrian section of Mitropoleos Street (aka "Kebab Street"), Thanasis spills out into Monastiraki Square, selling minced-meat souvlaki in a pita to go for 1.90€. Or eat at an outdoor table amid the throngs at this bustling corner of Plaka and the flea market. *69 Mitropoleos St.* ☎ *210/324-4705. $.*

10 **Tower of the Winds.** Built by astronomer Andronikos Kyristes, the octagonal 1st-century-B.C. Tower of the Winds at the end of Aiolou Street ("Street of the Winds"), inside the **Roman Agora** (a forum or market-place constructed under the reign of Julius Caesar and Augustus), depicts the eight wind deities. Once containing a water clock and topped by a weather vane, the area, Aerides, is named after this unique monument. In the 18th century, Whirling

Dervishes danced in the tower. The surrounding ruins of the Agora also contain the photogenic 15th-century **Fetiye** mosque, built to commemorate Mehmet II the Conqueror's visit to Athens in 1458, but you can't go in. ⏱ *20 min. Aiolou & Pelopida sts.* ☎ *210/324-5220 or 210/321-0185. Daily May–Oct 8am–7pm; Nov–Apr 8:30am–3pm; closed Jan 1, Mar 25, Easter Sunday, Ayiou Pnevmatos (Whit Monday), May 1 & Dec 25–26. Admission 2€ or w/Acropolis ticket. Metro: Monastiraki.*

11 ★★★ **Thission Open-Air Cinema.** The Thission cinema is one of the few places where you can still see a film under the stars in licensed comfort. Most cinemas like Thission have been declared cultural sites and cannot be used for any other purpose, but big cinema chains have also bought in, proving that outdoor theaters remain viable options, screening first-run as well as classic movies. Buy popcorn and a beer or glass of wine during the intermission, and bring them to your cafe table, interspersed between directors' chairs, in the breezy garden. See p 50.

The frieze atop the Tower of the Winds in the Roman Agora depicts Greek wind deities.

Shaded outdoor cafes along Iraklidon Street in Thissio are heated in winter and cooled in summer.

⑫ ★★★ Psyrri. Psyrri, favored by flower-selling Roma children, where bars and restaurants are crammed on narrow pedestrian streets, is the most lively of the central districts of Athens, positively hopping at night. You can sit outside and watch Athenians coming and going to and from their favorite night haunt or a *bouzouki*-filled (that is, accompanied by the traditional Greek guitar) dinner. *Iroon Square.*

⑬ Iraklidon Street. From Psyrri, walk to Iraklidon Street in Thissio (walk across Ermou St. and up the cobblestone walkway past the Thissio Metro station to Thissio Sq., and down Iraklidon), which is abuzz with outdoor cafe-bars. If it's winter, get cozy under a gas heater, and in summer cool off under mist machines and fans. Drinks are expensive, but you can sip (and sit) for hours. *Iraklidon & Apostolou Pavlou sts.*

⑭ ★★ Technopolis. If you hear muffled music as intermittent sound waves in Thissio, chances are there's a free open-air concert at Technopolis, the former gasworks and now exhibition-and-event space run by the city of Athens. The old brick smokestacks glow red at night and provide an orienting beacon, as does the Acropolis. Restaurants, cafe-bars, and clubs have sprung up in the surrounding (somewhat decrepit) area known as Gazi, now undergoing gentrification. ⏱ *2 hr. 100 Piraeos St. at Persefonis St.* ☎ *210/346-1589 or 210/346-7322. Metro: Kerameikos.*

Original 1857 gasworks pipes are now decoration for the Technopolis exhibition space in Gazi.

The Best **in Two Days**

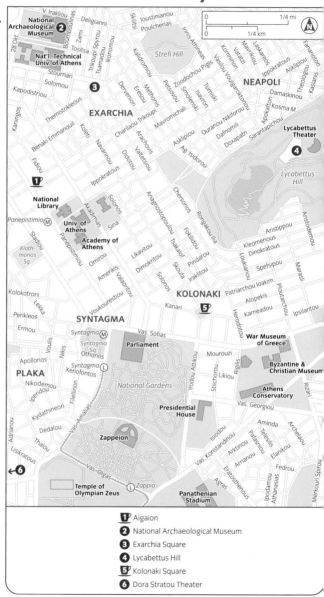

1 Aigaion
2 National Archaeological Museum
3 Exarchia Square
4 Lycabettus Hill
5 Kolonaki Square
6 Dora Stratou Theater

You can't come all the way to Athens and skip the museums. (Well, you could, but you would be missing an opportunity to fully explore the culture of a city not uncommonly called the "Cradle of Western Civilization.") The National Archaeological Museum in particular is considered one of the world's great collections, housing stunning Mycenaean antiquities, Cycladic sculptures, and Minoan frescoes, and your second day should be primarily devoted to it (it will probably take half the day). This one really is worth the trip.

START: **Metro to Omonia.**

The bronze statue of a horse and jockey in the National Archaeological Museum was recovered from a shipwreck off Cape Artemision.

1 **Aigaion.** Fill up at Aigaion, an Athenian institution, where you can sit in an old-fashioned, cafeteria-like basement to eat the specialty of the house, *loukoumades* (just-out-of-the-deep-fryer doughnut holes drizzled in honey and sprinkled with cinnamon). Cheese pies or homemade rice puddings and custard creams are also on the very limited menu (that's all they make). If sitting inside doesn't appeal, take it to go for 2.90€, or buy it by the kilo (18€ for 2.2 lb.) and gorge en route. *46 Panepistimiou St.* ☎ *210/ 381-4621 or 381-4622. $.*

2 ★★★ **National Archaeological Museum.** Most recently renovated in 2004 following damage from a 1999 earthquake and in anticipation of the Olympic Games, the fine archaeological specimens of this ancient civilization's giant legacy are housed in a handsome 1880 neoclassical building. It has had many alterations, but the facade is courtesy of Ernst Ziller. The museum is divided into sections—the prehistoric collection, the Santorini findings, sculptures, vases and minor objects, metallurgy, the Stathatos collection, the Vlastos collection, Egyptian art, and Near Eastern antiquities—and works range from the Neolithic period (8500–5500 B.C.) to the late Roman (1st century B.C.). Highlights include Trojan artifacts excavated by German treasure hunter Heinrich Schliemann, Mycenaean gold work (also uncovered by Schliemann), and Cycladic sculptures.

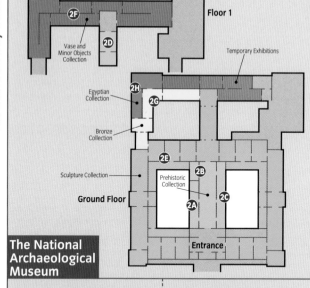

Floor 1

2F Vase and Minor Objects Collection

2D

Temporary Exhibitions

2H Egyptian Collection

2G

Bronze Collection

2E

Sculpture Collection

2B Prehistoric Collection

2A

2C

Ground Floor

Entrance

The National Archaeological Museum

The museum's **2A Neolithic Collection** houses ceramic pottery and figurines that date from 6800 B.C. Grouped with the Neolithic is the **2B Mycenaean Collection,** highlighted by the golden "Mask of Agamemnon" death mask. This royal funeral mask, uncovered in a grave at Mycenae, may actually be too old to have belonged to Agamemnon, who led the Greeks in battle to Troy. Follow this collection to the razor-planed marble figurines of the **2C Cycladic Collection.** Amazingly, these modern-looking milky-white statues were carved some 4,000 to 5,000 years ago. The **2D Thera Collection** of circa-1700-B.C. frescos from Akrotiri, on the isle of Santorini, emphasize that volcanically preserved settlement's connection to Minoan Crete: For an island town, Akrotiri—Greece's own Pompeii—had a wide network of external relations. The large **2E Sculpture Collection** shows the progression from the wooden

Egyptian to the fluid Classical, the angular to the anatomically correct. Also upstairs, represented in the **2F Vase and Minor Objects Collection,** are the famed red and black figures from Attic pottery. Exquisite jewelry and silver are also found here. The **2G Metals Collection** contains the bronze *Horse and Jockey* and *Poseidon (or Zeus)* of *Artemision* statues, from the 2nd century B.C. There is also a Virgin Mary look-alike, the *Lady of Kalymnos.* Finally, the **2H Egyptian Collection** covers that civilization from 5000 B.C. up to the Roman conquest. ⏱ *3 hr. 44 Patission & 28 Oktovriou sts.* ☎ *210/821-7717. May–Sept Mon 1–7:30pm; Tues–Sun & holidays 8am–7:30pm. Oct–Apr Mon 1–7:30pm; Thurs 8:30am–7:30pm; Tues–Wed, Fri–Sun & holidays 8:30am–3pm. Admission 7€ adults, 18 & under free, discounts for students, seniors. Metro: Victoria or trolley: 2, 3, 4, 5, 6, 7, 8, 9, 11, 13, 15.*

The November 17 Uprising

One of Greece's most recent dark periods was the 1967 coup by a group of midranking colonels. The military junta that took over the nation where democracy was born was both absurd—there were laws against miniskirts and long hair—and brutal. Secret police, torture, imprisonment, and exile were common practices of the despised, and infamously American-backed, far-right dictatorship. In 1973, tanks invaded the campus of the Polytechnic where students were protesting, leaving some 34 dead. It is commemorated each year—giving opportunistic anarchists more chances to vent—with a march on the massive U.S. embassy, while the date has also been adopted as the moniker of Greece's deadliest leftist terrorist group.

3 Exarchia Square. If you don't want to head back to your hotel for a rest, walk to the nearby student zone of Exarchia. This area's proximity to the Polytechnic and its anarchic reputation make it a magnet for artists (both fine and graffiti) and intellectuals, as well as students, who frequent the cafe-bars around the square. Also check out the interesting Boho shops, especially on Themistokleous, Emmanouil Benaki, and Zoodochou Pigis streets. *Stournari & Themistokleous sts.*

4 ★ kids Lycabettus Hill. *See p 35,* **9** .

5 ★ Kolonaki Square. This posh area of central Athens is the definition of Athenian cafe society, where the restaurants facing the square don't seem to have changed since the 1960s, where the movers and shakers live, where beautiful people have to be seen, and where the arty items in basement shops look as if they're on display more to amuse the proprietors than to actually sell. If you want to be seen as well, **DaCapo** is a good spot, with fine coffees, snacks, and even cocktails. *1 Tsakalof St. 210/360-2497. $.*

6 ★★ Dora Stratou Theater. One of the most unusual experiences is to see Greek folk costume dancing in the outdoor theater on Filopappou Hill. It's an adventure to walk there, and it's memorable to watch and listen to the live singers and musicians as you're sitting under the stars. Look out for (increasingly rare) bats as they dart in and out of the light. *See p 122.*

The wealthy, chic Kolonaki neighborhood of Athens, home to Kolonaki Square, is located on the southwestern slopes of Lycabettus Hill.

The Best **in Three Days**

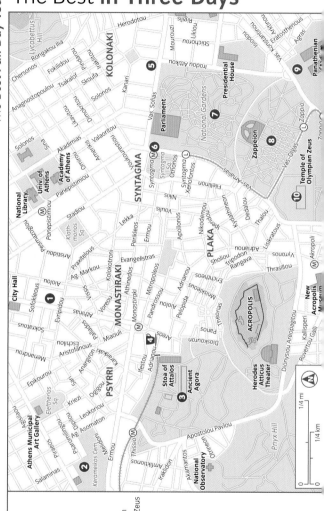

1. Central Market
2. Keramelkos
3. Ancient Agora
4. Dioskouri
5. Benaki Museum
6. Syntagma Station
7. National Gardens
8. Zappeion Gardens
9. Panathenian Stadium
10. Temple of Olympian Zeus

S tart your day at Athens's main farmers' market, on bustling Athinas Street, which used to be known for its bordellos and confidence men (who still play the occasional game of three-card Monte on the sidewalk), and pick up some dried fruit or nuts to carry you over till mealtime. Then detour to the ancient cemetery of Kerameikos, wander around the picturesque Ancient Agora, and make your way to a museum, walking back through the National Gardens to the all-marble stadium where the first Olympics were held and Zeus's temple. In the evening, hit the spots you missed on the other evenings. START: **Metro to Omonia.**

1 ★★ **Central Market.** Farmers' markets abound in neighborhoods around town (on Fri on Xenokratous St. in Kolonaki, and Zacharitsa or Matrozou sts. in Koukaki), but the main meat, fish, and vegetable market of Athens is here on Athinas Street near Omonia Square 6 days a week. If you're not in a protein mood, it also offers cheeses, dried nuts, and herbs, among other things. It opens at 6am, so you can start your day here. *See p 79.*

2 **Kerameikos.** If you have time, continue down Athinas Street to Ermou Street, and take Ermou west to this site, which includes the Sacred Gate, funerary avenues of graves, and monuments of famous

A stand at the Central Market on Athinas Street, home to 108 butchers, 150 seafood stands, and 80 fruit and vegetable stalls.

A kylix (drinking cup) in Attic red-figure style, on display at the Ancient Agora museum.

ancient Athenians. (Pericles delivered his funeral oration for the soldiers of the Peloponnesian War here in 431 B.C. In reference to Athens's constitution, he said, "We are rather a pattern to others than imitators ourselves.") The on-site museum houses organized exhibits with interesting finds, mainly related to burial customs, such as urns and monuments. *See p 61,* **11**.

3 ★ **kids** **Ancient Agora.** You can either zip through this marketplace of antiquity or chill out and write postcards here using an Acropolis ticket coupon. Once the center of commercial life in ancient Athens, with temples, gymnasiums, odeons, markets, and council houses where the *vouli* (parliament) legislated for the world's first democracy, broken columns are now strewn among crumbling foundations interspersed with olive, pink oleander, cypress, and palm trees.

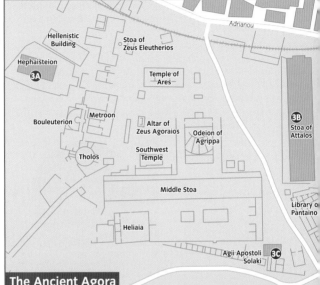

Hellenistic Building

Stoa of Zeus Eleutherios

Adrianou

Hephaisteion
3A

Temple of Ares

Bouleuterion

Metroon

Altar of Zeus Agoraios

Odeion of Agrippa

3B
Stoa of Attalos

Southwest Temple

Tholos

Middle Stoa

Library of Pantaino

Heliaia

Agii Apostoli Solaki **3C**

The Ancient Agora

Communal life in early Athens revolved around the Ancient Agora, although you'd be hard-pressed to reconstruct the layout of this market from the mind's eye. The **3A Hephaisteion,** better known as the Thisseion (which dates to 449–447 B.C.), is one of the world's best-preserved Greek temples due to protection from the Greek Orthodox Church, which used it from the 7th century to 1834 as its own house of worship. The circa-1950s **3B Stoa of Attalos** is a reconstruction of the 2nd-century-B.C. version, where businesses set up shop, philosophers debated, and people just hung out. The Stoa museum contains fascinating artifacts that show how the ancients carried out early democratic processes. Jurors voted by ballot: They cast a bronze disc with a solid axle if they believed that the defendant was innocent, and they cast a hollow one if they believed he was guilty. A marble *kleroterion*, an early

version of the lotto machine, was used to select citizens for jury duty. The **3C Agii Apostoli Solaki** is the only other structure intact, and justifiably so, as this church wasn't built until the 11th century. Everything else was demolished by either the invading Herulians in A.D. 267 or the subsequent private housing put up during the Roman and Byzantine eras. The area was still residential through the 1950s, when it was razed again—to dig for archaeological remnants of the original Agora. ⏱ *1 hr. Entrance/exit on Adrianou St. & Agiou Filippou, Monastiraki; west end of Polygnotou St., Plaka; & Thissio Sq., Thissio.* ☎ *210/321-0185. www.culture.gr. May–Oct Tues–Sun 8am–7pm, Mon 11am–7pm; reduced winter hours (3pm closing). Closed Jan 1, Mar 25, Easter Sunday, Ayiou Pnevmatos (Whit Monday), May 1 & Dec 25–26. Site & museum 4€ adults. Metro: Monastiraki or Thissio.*

4 **Dioskouri.** Go to the promenade behind (south of) Monastiraki station across from the Metro line that runs to Thissio, and your reward will be a view of the Acropolis above the Ancient Agora—and the low prices at this *meze*-restaurant and cafe that is always full. Look for the ancient-ship logo on the awnings (the sign's only in Greek). *37 & 39 Adrianou St.* ☎ *210/325-3323 or 325-3333. $$.*

5 ★★ **Benaki Museum.** Housed in the mansion of one of Athens's most prominent families, this excellent private museum contains artifacts from the Neolithic era to the 20th century. The folk-art collection (including costumes and icons) is superb, as are two rooms decorated in the style of 18th-century northern Greek mansions, with ancient bronzes, gold cups, Fayum portraits, and rare, early Christian textiles. A new wing has doubled the exhibition space of the early-20th-century neoclassical house, but the Benakis's massive collection of Islamic art must still be housed in a museum near the Thissio Metro station, and large exhibitions are held at its annex at 138 Piraeos St. (Bus: 049), which also has a gift shop/bookshop and cafe. ⏱ *1–2 hr. Koumbari & Vas. Sofias Ave.* ☎ *210/367-1000. www.benaki.gr. Admission 6€ adults, 3€ seniors, free on Thurs & for children 17 & under; see website for other discounts. Mon, Wed & Fri–Sat 9am–5pm; Thurs 9am–midnight; Sun 9am–3pm; closed Tues, holidays. Metro: Syntagma.*

A ceramic pitcher from the Benaki Museum, one of about 40,000 items on display there.

6 ★ **kids** **Syntagma Station.** There are archaeological finds from Metro excavations inside this station, but also stop at one of the open-air "museums" uncovered from the works. This one contains well-preserved Roman baths, with sections dating from the 5th and 3rd centuries A.D. ⏱ *10 min. Vas. Georgiou, Othonos & Filellinon sts. & Amalias Ave.*

7 **kids** **National Gardens.** The 16 hectares (40 acres) of crisscrossing paths, quiet little dead ends, and ponds among giant trees in the former Royal Gardens behind Parliament (once the palace) in the city center is a great place to escape the concrete jungle that surrounds it. Some 7,000 trees and 40,000 plants from Greece and abroad have taken root here since the mid-1800s, when Queen Amalia brought over a Bavarian gardener to redesign her backyard. It was nationalized in 1923. Stop at the **cafe**, 4 Irodou Attikou St. (☎ 210/ 723-2820), for refreshment. ⏱ *20 min. Syntagma Sq.; entrances from Zappeion Gardens, Amalias Ave. & Vas. Sofias & Irodou Attikou sts. Daily 8:30am–sunset.*

8 **Zappeion Gardens.** Adjacent to the National Gardens is the 14-hectare (35-acre) Zappeion, bequeathed in the 1880s by philanthropist Evangelias Zappas to kick-start the Olympic movement. Still resembling Henry Miller's "quintessence of park," it contains a small but important exhibition hall, a cafe-restaurant, and **Aigli,** Athens's oldest open-air cinema. You can still picture impressionistic, parasol-twirling women and children in sailor suits on the broad, tree-lined promenade, whose shade cools strolling Athenians on hot summer evenings, and the usual contingent of pensioners debating politics and playing *tavli* (backgammon). 🕐 *20 min. Entrances from the National Gardens, Amalias Ave. & Vas. Olgas & Vas. Konstantinou sts.*

9 Panathenian Stadium. Also called the Kalimarmaro ("beautiful marble") and Panathinaiko Stadium, it was reconstructed in marble by Herodes Atticus in A.D. 143–144, after the circa-330-B.C. original that hosted Panathenian games every 4 years. It was again rebuilt, for the first modern Olympics, in 1896 by benefactor George Averof and today is the venue for major events, including the finish line for the (original) Marathon run. It measures 1 *stade* (600 Greek ft.), hence the word *stadium,* and origi-nally held 50,000 people—the same as the Roman Coliseum. Unfortu-nately, you can no longer go in, but you can observe it from the facing square. For the 2004 **Olympic Stadium,** 37 Kifissias Ave. (☎ 210/683-4060; www.oaka.com.gr), with the beautiful roof by Spaniard Santi-ago Calatrava, head to Irini Metro

A detail of a Corinthian capital from the Temple of Olympian Zeus.

station. 🕐 *10 min. Vas. Konstantinou & Irodou Atikou sts.*

10 Temple of Olympian Zeus. Finish with a stop at Greece's largest temple, which took some 650 years to build between 515 B.C. and A.D. 132. It measures 96 by 40m (315 by 131 ft.) but only 15 of the original 104 columns are still standing, each 17m (56 ft.) high. 🕐 *45 min. Vas. Olgas St. & Amalias Ave. ☎ 210/922-6330. www.culture.gr. Admission 2€ or part of Acropolis ticket. Daily 8am–5pm; Apr–Oct 8am–7:30pm. Metro: Syn-tagma or Acropoli.* ●

The Zappeion exhibition hall in the Zappeion Gardens is symmetrically arranged around a circular interior atrium.

Athens **for Museum Lovers**

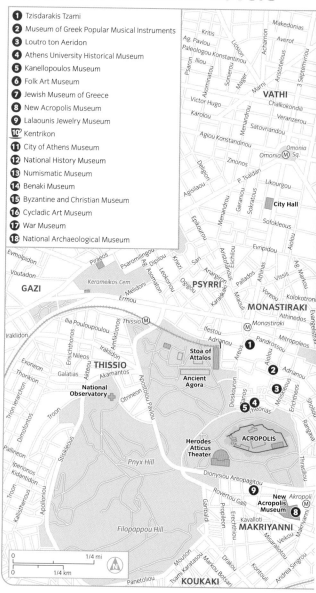

1. Tzisdarakis Tzami
2. Museum of Greek Popular Musical Instruments
3. Loutro ton Aeridon
4. Athens University Historical Museum
5. Kanellopoulos Museum
6. Folk Art Museum
7. Jewish Museum of Greece
8. New Acropolis Museum
9. Lalaounis Jewelry Museum
10. Kentrikon
11. City of Athens Museum
12. National History Museum
13. Numismatic Museum
14. Benaki Museum
15. Byzantine and Christian Museum
16. Cycladic Art Museum
17. War Museum
18. National Archaeological Museum

Previous page: The mosaic of the Madonna and Child at the door of the circa-11th-century Kapnikarea church on Ermou Street is actually a modern addition (from 1936).

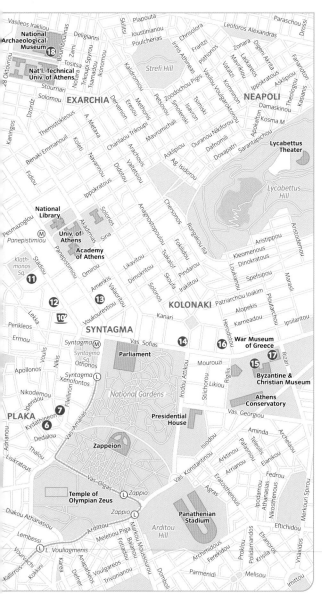

Greece coddles its culture: There are excellent state-run and private museums that are free or have low entrance fees. National museums and sites are free on Sundays and from November 1 to March 31 and on certain other days, but they close early; hours change in April and October. Check **www.culture.gr** or call ahead. START: **Metro to Monastiraki.**

Monastiraki and Plaka

1 Tzisdarakis Tzami. If you're curious about what that big 18th-century mosque—one of the remaining vestiges of 400 years of Ottoman rule—overlooking the square has inside, well, go in. (It's the Ceramic Folk Art Museum, by the way.) ⏲ *20 min. 1 Areos St. at Monastiraki Sq.* ☎ *210/324-2066. Wed–Mon 9am–2:30pm. Admission 2€. Metro: Monastiraki.*

2 ★ kids Museum of Greek Popular Musical Instruments. The Greek instruments here are informatively displayed with earphones to hear them. The museum, also a musicology center, features occasional performances (check the board.) ⏲ *30 min. 1–3 Diogenis St.* ☎ *210/325-0198. Tues, Thurs, Sun 10am–2pm; Wed noon–6pm. Admission free. Metro: Monastiraki.*

3 Loutro ton Aeridon. Roughly translated "Bathhouse of the Winds" (after Aeolus, god of wind), this is a 15th-century *hammam* (Turkish bath) restored as a museum. Buy the brochure (2€) for info in English, or listen to the 23-minute audio guide, skipping to room nos. 4 and 5 for evocative, firsthand accounts. ⏲ *15–30 min. 8 Kyrisstou St. Wed–Mon 9am–2:30pm. Metro: Monastiraki.*

4 Athens University Historical Museum. The pre-Ottoman residence of town planner and architect Stamatis Kleanthis, it was where the first classes for Athens's oldest university were held, though only for 4 years (1837–41), after which classes moved to the still-used Panepistimiou Street location. Beautifully restored, it contains various items relating to the history of

The Tzisdarakis Tzami mosque, now home to the Ceramic Folk Art Museum, faces Monastiraki Square.

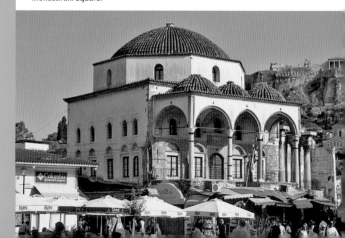

Greece's National and Kapodistrian University of Athens. ⏱ *30 min. 5 Tholou St. at Klepsydras St. ☎ 210/368-9502 or 210/368-9504. www.history-museum.uoa.gr. Mon–Fri 9:30am–2:30pm; June 1–Sept 30 Tues & Thurs–Fri 9:30am–2:30pm, Mon & Wed 9:30am–2:30pm & 6–9pm. Admission free. Metro: Monastiraki.*

❺ **Kanellopoulos Museum.** See a panorama of Greek art on a small scale: Art from the Hellenistic to post-Byzantine periods, a 2nd-century-B.C. marble head of Alexander the Great (356–323 B.C.), 17th- to 19th-century jewelry and weapons, Byzantine icons, and other objects are displayed in this beautiful, neoclassical building on the way to the Acropolis. ⏱ *30 min. 12 Theorias St. at Panos St. ☎ 210/321-2313. Tues–Sun 8:30am–3pm. Admission 2€. Metro: Monastiraki.*

A bust of Alexander the Great, king of Macedonia and conqueror of most of the Greek-known world, in the Kanellopoulos Museum.

❻ **Folk Art Museum.** It looks like it hasn't been updated since 1973, but the displays of modern Greek objects here are charming. Upstairs are nice collections of traditional buckles and costumes, with maps of where they're from, but the star is the complete room of frescoes by naïve artist Theophilos Hatzimihail. ⏱ *30–45 min. 17 Kydathineon St. ☎ 210/322-9031. Tues–Sun 9am–2pm. Admission 2€. Metro: Syntagma.*

❼ **Jewish Museum of Greece.** Jewish communities in Greece have been present since Hellenistic times, or at least since the Spanish Inquisition. Here, some 8,000 remnants of Greek Jewish life spanning 4,000 years have been amassed, including 600-year-old textiles, with displays on nine (small) levels. ⏱ *30–45 min. 39 Nikis St. ☎ 210/322-5582. www.jewish museum.gr. Mon–Fri 9am–2:30pm; Sun 10am–2pm. Admission 5€, students 3€. Metro: Syntagma.*

Makriyanni

❽ ★★ **kids New Acropolis Museum.** This sleek and minimalist new building houses sculptures and fragments, including frieze fragments and Caryatids ("maiden" columns), from the original Acropolis. See p 11, ❹.

❾ ★ **Lalaounis Jewelry Museum.** Not only jewelry lovers will feast over prolific designer Ilias Lalaounis's gold collection inspired by different epochs and cultures. ⏱ *30–45 min. 4 Karyatidon & 12 Kallisperi sts. ☎ 210/922-1044. Mon & Thurs–Sat 9am–4pm; Wed 9am–9pm; Sun 11am–4pm. Admission 3€. Metro: Akropoli or bus: 230.*

Center

🔟 **Kentrikon.** Come in off the streets to the arcade beside the shoe store (under the big KENTRIKON sign) to this old-fashioned, lunch-only (Mon–Sat noon–6pm) diner in the middle of the shopping district, where you can get a full meal or just stop for a drink. Long menu, good food, unpretentious service. *3 Kolokotroni St. (opposite the National History Museum in the arcade). ☎ 210/323-2482. $$.*

An icon of Christ removed from the cross, at the Byzantine and Christian Museum.

11 City of Athens Museum. This modest 1830s home of King Otto and Queen Amalia (where they lived while the royal palace/Parliament was being built) re-creates life in the royal household and features a superb collection from Byzantine times to the 19th

The neoclassic Iliou Melathron mansion, with its Ionic colonnades, is home to the Numismatic Museum.

century, including foreigners' impressions of Athens at population 25,000 (now 4 million). ⏱ *30–45 min. 7 Paparigopoulou St.* ☎ *210/323-1397. www.athenscitymuseum.gr. Mon & Wed–Fri 9am–4pm; Sat–Sun 10am–3pm. Admission 3€. Metro: Panepistimiou.*

12 National History Museum. Known as the *Palaia Vouli*, or Old Parliament (used 1875–1935), it shows Greece's history from the fall of Constantinople (1453) to World War II. Byron's (supposed) helmet and sword rest here. ⏱ *30–45 min. 13 Stadiou St. at Kolokotroni St.* ☎ *210/323-7617. Tues–Sun 9am–2pm. Admission 3€. Metro: Syntagma.*

13 Numismatic Museum. Entering via a pretty courtyard, Iliou Melathron ("Ilium Mansion") was eccentric excavator Heinrich Schliemann's home. It now attractively displays some 600,000 coins dating from 700 B.C. ⏱ *30 min. 12 Panepistimiou St.* ☎ *210/364-3774. Tues–Sun 8:30am–3pm. Admission 3€. Metro: Syntagma.*

Kolonaki/Evangelismos
14 ★★ Benaki Museum. Anthony Benakis collected artifacts over 35 years, then donated his house and collection to the state in

1931. It features antiquities, costumes, Asia Minor relics, and El Grecos, plus Lord Byron and War of Independence memorabilia. The gift shop has reproductions in silver and terra-cotta, jewelry, books, and icons. *See p 21,* ⑤.

⑮ Byzantine and Christian Museum.
Finds and history of the early Church are displayed in the new wings of the Tuscan-style 1848 villa of Sophie de Marbois, duchess de Plaisance (1785–1854), showing the transition from paganism to Christianity, with a few representations of the lyre-playing animal-lover Orpheus as Christ. ⏱ *1 hr. 22 Vasilissis Sofias Ave.* ☎ *210/721-1027. www. byzantinemuseum.gr. Apr–Sept Tues–Sun 8am–7:30pm; Oct–Mar Tues–Sun 8:30am–3pm. Admission 4€. Metro: Evangelismos.*

⑯ ★★ Cycladic Art Museum.
This private museum with the grand corner entrance has one of the best collections of Cycladic and ancient art dated 3200 to 2000 B.C., donated by Nicolas and Aikaterini Goulandris. The galleries are small and well lit. You'll likely enter via the **Stathatos Mansion,** 1 Herodotou

The Cup Bearer sculpture at the Cycladic Art Museum is attributed to the sophisticated Cycladic civilization, an amalgamation of Anatolian and Greek cultures.

St. at Vas. Sofias Avenue (☎ 210/ 722-8321 or 210/722-8323), which has retained its turn-of-the-century decor and is used to host temporary exhibits. ⏱ *1 hr. 4 Neophytou Douka St.* ☎ *210/722-8321 or 210/722-8323. www.cycladic.gr. Mon, Wed & Thurs–Fri 10am–4pm; Sat 10am–3pm. Admission 3.50€, Sat 1.80€. Metro: Syntagma or Evangelismos.*

⑰ kids War Museum.
Nothing like calling a spade a spade, this cheerful armed-forces museum has a collection from Greece's military past, from antiquity to the 20th century. The exhibits include battle plans, weaponry, uniforms (including a samurai outfit), etchings, aircraft, and memorabilia from philhellenes who came to fight in the 19th-century War of Independence (from the Ottomans), and who cheered again when Greece scored the first victory against an Axis power (Italy) in World War II. ⏱ *1 hr. 2 Rizari St. at Vas Sofias Ave.* ☎ *210/ 724-4464. Tues–Sun 9am–2pm. Free admission. Metro: Evangelismos.*

Museo/Exarchia/Omonia

⑱ ★★★ National Archaeological Museum.
See p 15, ②.

Poseidon of Artemision, at the National Archaeological Museum, more likely depicts Zeus, according to archaeologists.

Holidays in Athens

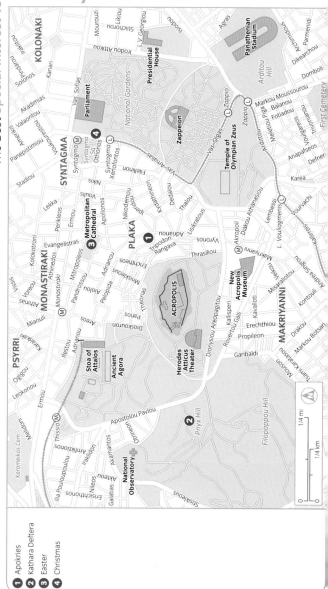

1 Apokries

2 Kathara Deftera

3 Easter

4 Christmas

If you're lucky to be here during a major holiday, expect some hassle and a lot of fun. Greeks are an observant bunch, so businesses may shut down and Athenians living abroad may return home for the celebrations (especially during Easter week)—but although sites may be closed and transportation and lodging a bit more expensive during the major holidays, you'll find feasts and festivities all over town. The major ones are highlighted here. START: **Metro to Syntagma.**

1 ★ kids **Apokries.** This pre-Lent Carnival is a rollicking time in Athens. Parades take place on weekends in some municipalities, and kids dress up in costumes and "promenade" with their parents, all culminating in last-night-before-Lent mayhem: In **Plaka,** this means good-natured head-bopping with plastic bats. See p 11, **6**.

2 ★★ kids **Kathara Deftera.** On this, the first day of Lent (Clean Monday), you'll see a lot of stray kites caught in trees, and more in the air (a tradition on Kathara Deftera), especially around Filopappou Hill, where the Lenten fast officially begins. Try your luck at flying your own kite from **Pnyx Hill;** bring a picnic snack lunch of canned octopus, dolmades (rice-stuffed grapevine leaves), and other Lenten foods and, of course, a kite (sold everywhere). ⏱ *1–2 hr. Dionysiou Areopagitou/Apostolou Pavlou sts. Metro: Thissio.*

3 ★★★ **Easter.** The most important date on the Christian Orthodox calendar (in Greek, *Pascha,* like "paschal") is particularly moving. It lasts a week (most people fast), culminating in a feast of lamb-on-the-spit wherever it can be accommodated, from backyards and summer homes to Athens carports, apartment roof terraces, and parks. Church bells toll on Good Friday, and the day ends with a candlelit procession behind the *epitaphios* (funeral bier) through parish streets at about

8pm. To partake, be outside a church with a taper at midnight on Saturday to receive the flame from Jerusalem, signaling Christ's resurrection. You'll also hear a lot of fireworks.

4 ★★★ kids **Christmas.** Athens is a decadent visual feast at this magic time, when the city puts on a fantastic display. Streets, squares, and trees are decked out in lights; and displays, concerts, and events, particularly at central **Syntagma Square** (see p 59, **1**) and inside the **National Gardens** (see p 21, **7**), tempt adults and children. Look for special packages, as luxe hotels and top restaurants vie to offer the most sumptuous menu for Christmas and New Year's Eve.

Children dress in costume for Carnival, the last opportunity for excess before Lent begins.

Athens **with Kids**

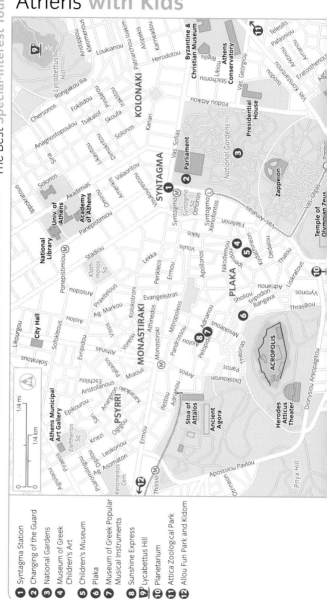

1 Syntagma Station
2 Changing of the Guard
3 National Gardens
4 Museum of Greek Children's Art
5 Children's Museum
6 Plaka
7 Museum of Greek Popular Musical Instruments
8 Sunshine Express
9 Lycabettus Hill
10 Planetarium
11 Attica Zoological Park
12 Allou Fun Park and Kidom

Children are practically worshiped in Greece, and you can take them almost anywhere (the concept of a neighborhood babysitter is nonexistent), including tavernas, restaurants, and alcohol-serving cafe-bars. However, the sidewalks in Athens are not stroller-friendly; most people use the roads. Keep this in mind as you follow the tour below, which includes age-appropriate activities for tikes through teens. START: **Metro to Syntagma.**

1 ★ kids Syntagma Station.
Show older kids the antiquities inside and outside the Metro station on Amalias Avenue, opened in 2000, which provides a window into more than 25 centuries of the city's buried past. They will enjoy the layers of the ancient city discovered during construction, particularly the graves and the remains of an ancient aqueduct used to bring water from Mount Hymettus to Athens in the 5th century B.C. Outside are 1,800-year-old Roman baths covered by a nonglare glass roof—one of several open-air free museum exhibits around the center displaying finds uncovered during Metro works. In addition, children will probably just enjoy riding the train. ⏱ *45 min. Amalias Ave. & Vas. Georgiou St. Daily 5:30am–midnight. Metro: Syntagma.*

2 ★★ kids Changing of the Guard. In front of Parliament at Syntagma Square, two *Evzones* (traditionally dressed soldiers of the Presidential Guard) keep watch at the Tomb of the Unknown Soldier. Every hour on the hour (you can feed the ubiquitous pigeons while you wait), the guards do some pretty fancy footwork in front of the tomb. A much more elaborate duty-rotation ceremony occurs on Sunday at 11am. ⏱ *15 min. Amalias Ave. & Vas. Georgiou St. Metro: Syntagma.*

3 kids National Gardens. The one-time Royal Gardens is the city's great escape. Wander along trails lined with some 500 plant varieties (learn more about them at the

Soldiers in foustanella *and other military uniforms salute at the Tomb of the Unknown Soldier in Syntagma Square.*

Botanical Museum on the grounds; ☎ 210/721-1178) to the duck and turtle ponds, the small zoo (birds, wild goats, and a donkey), and beyond, and then rest on benches or at the **cafe,** 4 Irodou Attikou St. (☎ 210/723-2820). Children can read, play chess, or paint at the **"child library"** (☎ 210/323-6503); the librarian will babysit if the tots can quietly do their thing. Continue through to the **Zappeion Gardens** (see p 21, **8**) and the **Panathenian Stadium** (see p 22, **9**). *See p 21,* **7**.

4 kids Museum of Greek Children's Art. School art-contest winners aged 4 to 14 from Greece and elsewhere are on colorful display

Children of Greece

Children may be put on a pedestal in Athens, but they are generally catered to through private ventures rather than public. There may be a lot of public playgrounds, but they are poorly maintained. Instead, most parents take their children to the local square when the siesta and heat of the day are over, at around 7pm in summer. On the other hand, state-run childcare centers accept children as young as 40 days old free of charge for working mothers, and education is free for every Greek citizen right through to university.

here. There's also an interesting selection of original postcards and workshops where your kids can paint their own masterpieces. 🕐 *20 min. 9 Kodrou St. at Voulis St.* 📞 *210/331-2621. www.childrensart museum.gr. Tues–Sat 10am–2pm; Sun 11am–2pm; closed Mon, holidays, Aug. Adults 2€, free for children. Metro: Syntagma.*

5 ★ **kids Children's Museum.** This lively museum features exhibits combined with activity space where young children can experiment and create (cast shadows, blow bubbles, draw, and so on). Some Greek-made

toys are available at the shop. 🕐 *1 hr. 14 Kydathineon St.* 📞 *210/331-2995. www.hcm.gr. Tues–Fri 10am–2pm; Sat–Sun 10am–3pm. Free admission. Metro: Syntagma.*

6 ★★★ **kids Plaka.** The area of Anafiotika in Plaka is like an island village. In fact, it was named for the islanders of Anafi who originally came to Athens to build the king's palace in the 19th century. Children will enjoy wandering through the narrow streets. 🕐 *1 hr. Various approaches; one is from Stratonos St. Metro: Syntagma or Akropoli.*

An exhibit of paintings by winners of a children's art contest is displayed at the Museum of Greek Children's Art.

7 ★ kids **Museum of Greek Popular Musical Instruments.** Kids with a musical bent will like this museum, where they can listen to the tambourines, lutes, lyres, drums, and clarinets on display. *See p 26,* **2**.

8 ★ kids **Sunshine Express.** Save tiring little legs, get your bearings, and pass the main sites of Athens at the same time by boarding this *trenaki* (little train), which makes a circuit around pedestrian central roads (on car tires, not a track). An alternative is the **Athens Happy Train,** Ermou Street at Syntagma Square (☎ 210/725-5400). ⌚ *40 min. Terminal: Aiolou & Adrianou sts.* ☎ *210/881-9252. www. sunshine-express.gr. Winter Sat–Sun & holidays 11am to dark; summer Mon–Fri 11:30am–2:30pm & 5pm–midnight, Sat–Sun 11am–midnight. Adults 5€, children 9 & under 3€. Metro: Monastiraki.*

9 ★ kids **Lycabettus Hill.** Take the **teleferik** (cable car) up this 295m (965-ft.) hill for a fabulous view of the city, and have a (rather expensive) ice cream (10€) at the **cafe** on top. Then run or walk back down the hill on one of the many paths. Buses 022, 060, and 200 go near the base station, but it's a hard uphill hike just to get to that point. (Take the bus from Akademias St., Kanari St., or Kolonaki Sq. and get off at Loukianou or Marasli sts.) *Teleferik: Aristippou & Ploutarchou sts.* ☎ *210/721-0701. Daily every 30 min. 9am–3am. Adults 5.50€ round-trip, 2.80€ one-way, children 7 & under 2.75€ (no credit cards). Bus: 022, 060 & 200.*

10 ★ kids **Planetarium.** Reopened in 2003 with a 25m (82-ft.) large-format iWerks (like IMAX) dome screen—10 times larger than conventional cinema projections and more than two basketball courts in size—

The iguana, here finishing a meal at the Attica Zoological Park, has a photoreceptive third eye on its head.

the 40-minute productions here take the audience on intergalactic (or undersea, or overland) journeys with a 360-degree view. ⌚ *1 hr. Eugenides Institute, 387 Syngrou.* ☎ *210/946-9600. www.eugenfound.edu.gr. Adults 6€ (regular screen) or 8€ (big screen), children & university students w/ID 4€ & 5€, respectively. Bus: 126, B2, A2 (from Akadimias St.), 550.*

11 ★★★ kids **Attica Zoological Park.** This zoo houses the third-largest collection of birds in the world, and a herd of endangered native horses. Little ones can even ride a pony. *See p 84,* **1**.

12 kids **Allou Fun Park and Kidom.** In out-of-the-way Rendi (20 min. away by bus), this big amusement park has a lot of rides—and not just for teens. Adrenaline pumpers include the 40m (131-ft.) drop Shock Tower. Kidom is for the little ones. ⌚ *1–2 hr. Kifissou & Petrou Ralli aves., Agios Ioannis–Rendi. Kidom:* ☎ *210/425-2600. Allou:* ☎ *210/425-6999. www.alloufunpark.gr. Mon–Thurs 5pm–1am; Fri 5pm–2am; Sat 10am–2am; Sun 10am–1am. Kidom (ages 3–9) closes at 11pm. Free entrance. Unlimited rides 23€; individual rides 3€–10€. Bus: B18, G18, or 21.*

Olde Athens

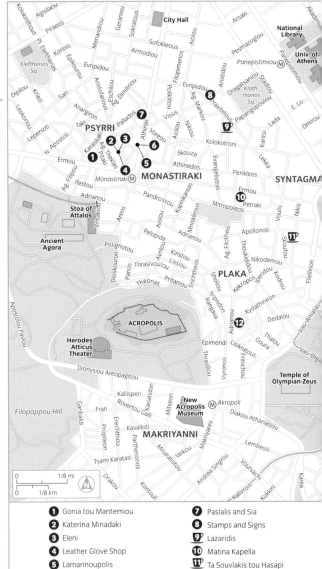

1. Gonia tou Mantemiou
2. Katerina Minadaki
3. Eleni
4. Leather Glove Shop
5. Lamarinoupolis
6. Kleidia o Kostis
7. Pasialis and Sia
8. Stamps and Signs
9. Lazaridis
10. Matina Kapella
11. Ta Souvlakis tou Hasapi
12. Roussos Art and Jewelry

ven today, numerous old-world craftsmen still front their own shops on the streets of this modern European capital. And while many thrive, some skills will die out for lack of apprentice interest, or because the wares can be imported cheaper. See, and better yet buy, from these charming places on the verge of extinction. Browsing is still welcomed in these shops—while it may be more difficult in larger establishments, where hired staff are expected to engage customers and try to make a sale, and do this by shadowing you (to "assist") as you look around. For the best of this nostalgic side of Athens life, start by walking through Psyrri and east of Athinas Street to Polykleitou, Praxitelous, Agiou Markou, and Perikleous. START: **Metro to Monastiraki.**

❶ Gonia tou Mantemiou. Many shops in the Psyrri area sell unique brightly painted tin-and-mesh boxes in various sizes (15€–60€) to keep picnic food in—and ants and other crawlies out. This one also sells fireplaces, with pails, watering cans, and boxes hanging from the ceiling. ⏱ *10 min. 98 Ermou St. at Artemidos St.* ☎ *210/321-7442. Metro: Monastiraki.*

❷ Katerina Minadaki. Katerina and her husband make beautiful soft leather and cloth handbags (60€–120€)—a rarity, as most of the craftsmen make only hard leather bags. They also make purses to order, but prefer to see an actual example of what you're looking for, rather than a photo. ⏱ *10 min. 3rd floor, 9 Miaouli St. (through the arcade).* ☎ *210/321-5903. Metro: Monastiraki.*

A workbench at Lamarinoupolis displays the tools of tinsmithing.

Handmade leather handbags and gloves on sale at Katerina Minadaki.

❸ Eleni. Prada? Gucci? Manolo Blahnik, anyone? Fashionistas who don't have the budget to match their tastes can get beautifully made designer-reproduction shoes for 100€ to 150€, made to order (allow 7–10 days) on the premises. Otherwise have a look in this store—they might just have a floor model in your size. ⏱ *10 min. 9 Miaouli St. (on the ground floor in the Singer arcade).* ☎ *210/322-7678. No credit cards. Metro: Monastiraki.*

❹ Leather Glove Shop. Gorgeous uptown-quality leather gloves can be bought for 20€ to 30€ here, if you're willing to venture up to the bright yellow fifth floor. Call ahead, as hours are erratic. ⏱ *10 min. 9 Miaouli St. (through the arcade).* ☎ *210/322-5701. Metro: Monastiraki.*

❺ Lamarinoupolis. Psyrri still has a few tinsmiths, where you can find original lightweight items, such as typical taverna barrel wine jugs, mini

Cow and goat bells hang from the ceiling of Kleidia o Kostis.

watering cans, and pails in all sizes (from 3€). Venture carefully down the steep steps to see more wares and the workshop. ⏱ *10 min. 17 Athinas & 2 Kakourgodikeiou sts. (beside Cyprus Bank).* ☎ *210/324-8345. No credit cards. Metro: Monastiraki.*

⑥ Kleidia o Kostis. You can find quaint handmade goat bells in varying sizes as souvenirs or as original house decorations (or, of course, as bells for your goat, if you have one—as is common in rural areas of Greece) from this tiny yellow-painted

A coffee latte at Lazaridis goes nicely with filo pastries.

key shop. The ceiling is full of bells. ⏱ *10 min. 17 Athinas St.* ☎ *210/ 321-0442. No credit cards. Metro: Monastiraki.*

⑦ Pasialis and Sia. This bric-a-brac shop with wares along the sidewalk will be renovated by the time you read this. The store sells all kinds of merchandise, from wine barrels to fake flowers to tin vases and wine jugs, as well as basketry and woven goods, including really handy reed slippers, which can be worn at the beach. ⏱ *10 min. 5 Pallados St.* ☎ *210/321-4200. Metro: Monastiraki.*

⑧ Stamps and Signs. If you like the old-fashioned, dual-language street signs common around the central tourist areas, get one specially made from a shop in this commercial triangle. Signs cost from 24€ and don't take long to make. ⏱ *20 min. 7 Evripidou St. at Klafthmonos Sq.* ☎ *210/323-5897. No credit cards. Metro: Panepistimiou.*

⑨ Lazaridis. Get a tasty *bougatsa* (cream-filled filo), or another Thessaloniki/Asia Minor–style "breakfast" sweet or pita (1.70€– 2€) here. And if you want to try *kazandibi*—a "burnt" rice-pudding confection—they have that, too. Sit at the high stool tables or take away. *25 Praxitelous St.* ☎ *210/322-5005. $.*

🔟 **Matina Kapella.** Shops like this make me really sad, especially when the owners are elderly and you just know the craft will die out when they retire. With such elegant veiled and pillbox hats on display, it's a shame these are now relegated to bridal or evening wear. Men and women can also get their winter caps here. A beret starts at 20€. 🕐 *10 min. 2 Fokionos St. at Ermou St.* ☎ *210/322-7817. Tues & Thurs–Fri 8am–8pm; Mon, Wed, Sat 8am–3pm. No credit cards. Metro: Syntagma.*

The hat selection on display at Matina Kapella.

11 **Ta Souvlakis tou Hasapi.** If you're in a real rush and want something more substantial than a *bougatsa,* get a kebab or gyro to go, or eat at the counter. This lunchtime outlet is popular, tasty, and fast. A single skewer of pork, chicken, or mince starts at 1.20€. *1 Apollonos St.* ☎ *210/322-0459. $.*

12 **Roussos Art and Jewelry.** For porcelain Greek dolls made at a workshop in western Athens, come here; they start at 40€. But it's also easy to find other handcrafted Greek-made trinkets from this shop located at the main Plaka intersection. 🕐 *10 min. 121 Adrianou St. at Kydathineon St.* ☎ *210/322-6395. Metro: Akropoli.*

Roussos Art and Jewelry sells handmade bronze statuettes of the Greek gods.

Architectural Athens

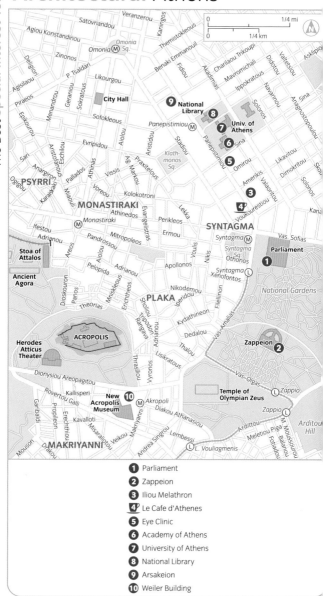

1. Parliament
2. Zappeion
3. Iliou Melathron
4. Le Cafe d'Athenes
5. Eye Clinic
6. Academy of Athens
7. University of Athens
8. National Library
9. Arsakeion
10. Weiler Building

The Athens basin may be a sprawl of ancient ruins, but the city has managed to protect the beautiful 19th- and early-20th-century buildings in the historic center. Central Panepistimiou Street, which connects Omonia and Syntagma squares, is the headquarters for many private enterprises and offers a great sampling of modern Greek architecture. START: **Metro to Syntagma.**

The striking Parliament building, on Syntagma Square, was formerly King Otto's palace.

1 Parliament. The biggest landmark in the city center, the 1842 former Royal Palace of Bavarian-born King Otto (1833–62), has Munich architects to blame for its plain neoclassical design, which prompted a *London Illustrated News* correspondent to lament "the ugliness of the palace. . . . It is invariably compared by travelers to a huge manufactory, while the interior plan is, if possible, in worse taste than the exterior." Then bigger than Buckingham Palace, its Pompeian-style decor was damaged in a 1909 fire. It has housed Greece's parliament since 1935. The **Tomb of the Unknown Soldier,** guarded by two highly photogenic soldiers in traditional *foustanellas* (ceremonial skirtlike garments), fronts the building. ⏱ *15 min. Amalias Ave. & Vas. Georgiou St. at Syntagma Sq. Metro: Syntagma.*

2 Zappeion. This semicircular exhibition hall is a classical public building associated with many historic events, such as the signing of Greece into the European Union. It was originally bankrolled by expat Evangelias Zappas in his quest to spark the modern Olympic Games, which took place after his death at the nearby Panathenian Stadium in 1896. The 1888 construction by Theophilos Hansen, the Athens Academy and Library architect, was plagued by indecision over its design. It was renovated in 1959 and remodeled in 1982 for Greece's EEC presidency. *See p 21,* **8**.

3 Iliou Melathron. Perhaps the best known of royal-court architect Ernst Ziller's numerous buildings, this Renaissance-style one behind swastika-adorned gates was built in 1878 for the excavator of Troy, Heinrich Schliemann, and named for that fabled city ("Ilium Mansion"). It is now the well-laid-out Numismatic Museum, which contains coins dating from 700 B.C. *See p 28,* **13**.

4 **Le Cafe d'Athenes.** Zonar's, a beloved aristocratic pastry shop, was closed in 2001, when the circa-1930s Attica Department Store building in which it resided was overhauled. Greece's Everest fast-food chain opened a copy in late 2007 to Athenians' delight, and it's now more packed (and posh) than ever. *Panepistimiou and Voukourestiou sts.* ☎ *210/321-1158. $$.*

5 **Eye Clinic.** The Ophthalmological Clinic (built 1847–51) was originally designed in a neoclassical style like the "neoclassical trilogy" of the Hansen brothers (the Academy, University, and Library), but was redesigned in the Byzantine style by Lissandros Kaftantzoglou at the request of King Otto. Another story was added in 1869 to keep the eye-diseased separate, so as not to infect other patients; more sections were built in 1881. It has belonged to the University of Athens's Faculty of Medicine since 1869. ⏱ *10 min. Panepistimiou & Sina sts. Metro: Panepistimiou.*

A statue of Kapodistrias, first president of the modern college, greets visitors to the University of Athens.

The ornate Public Meeting Hall of the Academy of Athens has murals that stretch for more than 50m (164 ft.).

6 **Academy of Athens.** Built in two phases (1859–63 and 1868–85), this neoclassical structure with its Ionic columns and entrance based on the eastern Erechtheum was built by royal-court architect Theophilos Hansen (1813–91). Bankrolled by Baron Georgios Sinas (1783–1856), who has a statue in the hall, is an example of mature (some would say mad) neoclassical design. Athena and Apollo top the columns. Only the (nonlending) library is open to the public. ⏱ *10 min. 28 Panepistimiou St.* ☎ *210/360-0207, 210/360-0209, or 210/364-2918. Metro: Panepistimiou.*

7 **University of Athens.** On Eleftherios Venizelos Street (its name in signs only; Panepistimiou, or "University," is how it's known to one and all), this plainer neoclassical building (compared to the Academy) was designed by Christian Hansen, Theophilos's brother. The portico is Ionic Pentelic marble, with frescoes of ancient Greek authors. The statues are of British prime minister William Gladstone, Ioannis Kapodistrias (the first modern president for

ΚΑΠΟΔΙΣΤΡΙΑΣ

whom the university is named), and other notables. ⏱ *10 min. 30 Panepistimiou St. No switchboard. www.uoa.gr. Metro: Panepistimiou.*

8 National Library. Another building designed by Theophilos Hansen (who also planned Viennese public buildings), and financed by Panagis Valianos (now a statue in front), this nonlending library of university and state holdings is another enthusiastic nod to antiquity. Built from 1887 to 1891 of Pentelic marble, it contains 10th- or 11th-century illuminated gospels. ⏱ *10 min. 32 Panepistimiou St. No switchboard. www.nlg.gr. Mon–Thurs 9am–8pm; Fri–Sat 9am–2pm. Metro: Panepistimiou.*

9 Arsakeion. Originally a girls' school founded by Apostolos Arsaki in 1836 (now a network of coed private schools throughout Greece), the neoclassical complex was rebuilt in 1848 by Greek architect Lissandros Kaftantzoglou, and again by Constantine Maroudis in the early 20th century. It now houses the Council of State, the Education Society, and a (quiet) book arcade. ⏱ *15 min. 47 Panepistimiou St. at Arsaki St.* ☎ *210/371-0097. www.ste.gr. Metro: Panepistimiou.*

The National Library, third in a trilogy of neoclassical buildings by the Hansen brothers.

10 Weiler Building. The circa-1834 Rundbogen-style building, now overwhelmed by the New Acropolis Museum, was designed as a military hospital by Wilhelm von Weiler, an architect in the Bavarian army. Used as both police and partisan army headquarters during the post–World War II civil war, it has been the Center for Acropolis Studies since 1987. ⏱ *10 min. 2–4 Makriyanni St.* ☎ *210/923-9381. Metro: Akropoli.*

Architecture in Brief

After Greece's 1821 War of Independence captured the imaginations of Romantic Victorians (during which avid "philhellenes" captured many Greek antiquities), the capital was moved to Athens from Nafplio. Bavarian King Otto and his architects planned for a town of 40,000, not 4 million—which explains the haphazard layout and crowded streets—with public buildings designed in the neoclassical style to honor the culture they idealized. The interwar period also saw Eclecticism, Art Nouveau, modernist, and Bauhaus architecture, and buildings taller than the usual two or three stories. The uniformly dull concrete blocks that dominate many neighborhoods, however, are the pragmatic result of a mass influx of rural migrants in the 1950s.

Byzantine Athens

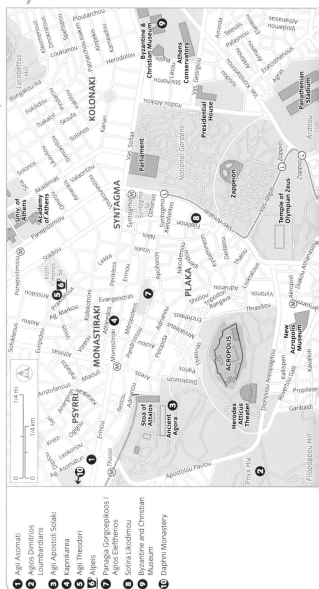

Athens is linked with the early Church, going back to the time of Christ (Paul preached here), and still has a large number of Eastern Orthodox houses of worship from what was formerly a small, provincial town in the Byzantine Empire. Progress has fortunately marched around rather than over many of these unique Attica-style churches, much to our gain. START: **Metro to Thissio.**

1 Agii Asomati. With an Athenian-style dome, this cruciform church from the 11th century sunken in the road at Ermou Street beside Thissio Metro station is eclectic but a bit forlorn. Its original Byzantine structure was altered in the 1950s, and it's rarely, if ever, open, with life going by around it as if it were invisible, just as its name ("Saints of the Disembodied") suggests. ⏱ *5 min. Agion Asomaton & Ermou sts. Metro: Thissio.*

2 ★★ Agios Dimitrios Loumbardiaris. The lovely 14th-century Church of St. James the Bombardier is nestled in a copse on Pnyx Hill. Legend tells that on October 26, 1645, the Ottoman commander of the Acropolis garrison, Yusuf Aga, planned to massacre Christians gathered here for name-day celebrations by bombarding the church with a cannon from the Propylaia on the Acropolis. The night before the attack, lightning exploded the gunpowder there, killing Aga and his family, except his Christian daughter. ⏱ *45 min. Apostolou Pavlou St., on the path opposite (south) the entrance to the Acropolis. Metro: Akropoli or bus: 230.*

3 Agii Apostoli Solaki. On the site of the Ancient Agora, this four-columned cruciform Church of the Holy Apostles of Solakis is a very early (ca. A.D.1020) and beautiful example of Athenian/Attic Byzantine architecture. Restored in the 1950s by the Samuel H. Kress Foundation of New York, it has pseudo-*kufic* (the oldest Arab calligraphy) decoration and, unusually, multiple apses (a semicircular and vaulted protruding part of the main building that usually houses the altar). The 17th-century wall paintings are from a demolished church. ⏱ *10 min. Dionysiou Areopagitou St., in the Ancient Agora. Metro: Monastiraki.*

Agii Apostoli Solaki church, with the National Observatory and Agia Marina in the background, was named for Christ's Apostles.

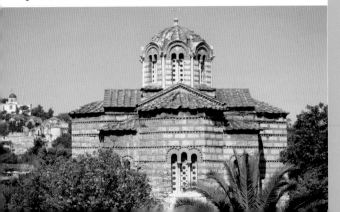

The Kapnikarea chapel is dedicated to the Virgin Mary, and a portrait of the Madonna and Child sits over the front entrance.

④ ★ Kapnikarea. The little 11th- to 13th-century church in the middle of Ermou Street near Monastiraki has Bavaria's King Ludwig (King Otto's father) to thank for its survival on the site of an ancient temple to Athena (or possibly Demeter; it's not known which), as town planners wanted to demolish it in 1834. The dome of this cruciform church is dedicated to the Virgin Mary. 🕐 *10 min. Ermou & Kapnikarea sts. Metro: Monastiraki.*

⑤ Agii Theodori. It's easy to bypass this circa-11th-century church on Evripidou Street, but it's one of the most beautiful, and built with much care on the site of another older structure. It was renovated in 1065, as marble tablets over the door attest, and sustained damage during the 19th-century War of Independence but was restored in 1840. 🕐 *10 min. Evripidou & Aristidou sts. at Klafthmonos Sq. Metro: Panepistimiou.*

⑥ Alpeis. Get a cheap, tasty souvlaki, full meal, or refreshment at this cafe, and sit outside in front of one of Athens's most beautiful Byzantine churches, Agii Theodori, on a pleasant square near the Central Market and Panepistimiou Street landmarks. *7 Palaion Patron Germanou St. at Klafthmonos Sq.* 📞 *210/331-0384.*

⑦ ★ Panagia Gorgoepikoos/ Agios Eleftherios. A small church dedicated to the Virgin Mary Gorgoepikoos ("she who hears quickly") and St. Eleftherios (patron saint of freedom), it is overpowered by the unremarkable, mid-1800s Metropolitan Cathedral next door. It was built in the late 12th century and constructed entirely with antiquities from an ancient temple founded some 400 years earlier on the site by Empress Irene. Also called the "little Metropolis," it was the official Episcopal See of Athens after Orthodox bishops were expelled by Franks and Ottomans in turn from the Parthenon, which they had converted into a church. Note the beautiful relief carvings of flora and fauna

The 11th-century Agii Theodori chapel has a domed, tiled Byzantine roof, common to many Christian churches in Athens.

An image of Christ Pantocrator ("Almighty") looks down from the ceiling of the Daphni monastery.

around the perimeter as well as inside, if you're lucky enough to pass by when it's open. ⏱ *10 min. Mitropoleos & Agias Filotheis sts. at Mitropoleos Sq. Metro: Monastiraki.*

8 Sotira Likodimou. Generally known as the "Russian Church" after the Russian Orthodox Church took over its administration, it is also known as the Church of St. Nicodemus. The Byzantine structure is the biggest medieval church in Athens. Founded prior to 1031 by Stefan Likodimou, it's a copy of Osios Loukas monastery in Boeotia. The Russians bought and restored the derelict church in the mid–19th century and added a bell tower, the bell being a gift from the czar. The interior was painted by noted Bavarian artist Ludwig Thiersch and Greek Nikiforos Lytras. ⏱ *10 min. 21 Filellinon St.* ☎ *210/323-1090. Metro: Syntagma.*

9 Byzantine and Christian Museum. *See p 29,* **15**.

10 Daphni Monastery. If only the walls could talk at this monastery, founded in the 6th century on the site of an ancient sanctuary. Originally a rare three-aisled basilica, it under-

went many structural changes: Ionic columns from the temple of Apollo (destroyed by Goths in A.D. 395) were used in its construction—and then removed by Lord Elgin (one remains). In the 11th century, it was dedicated to the Dormition of the Virgin. It became a monastery for Frankish Cistercian monks (rare in Greece) in the 1200s, it was returned to the Orthodox Church by the Turks in 1458, Greeks used it as a garrison during the 1820s War of Independence, and Bavarian troops camped out here when their king's son was installed a decade later. From 1883 to 1885, it was used as a psychiatric asylum. It suffered earthquake damage a few years later, when the site was also first excavated (1892). It is decorated with unique 11th-century mosaics. Daphni is located west of Athens and can be an ordeal to get to; allow plenty of time and check that it is open. (It was closed for restoration at the time of publication.) ⏱ *2 hr. Iera Odos, Attica.* ☎ *210/581-1558. www.culture.gr. Check website for hours. Bus: A16, B16, [gam]16, E16, E63, 801, 836, 845, 865, 866.*

Panagia Gorgoepikoos is built largely of marble and contains various Greek, Roman, Byzantine, and early Christian reliefs, paintings, and icons.

Romantic Athens

1. Parthenon
2. Plaka
3. Acropolis
4. Filopappou Hill
5. Grand Promenade
6. To Koutouki
7. Thission Open Air Cinema
8. Lycabettus Hill
9. Zappeion Gardens

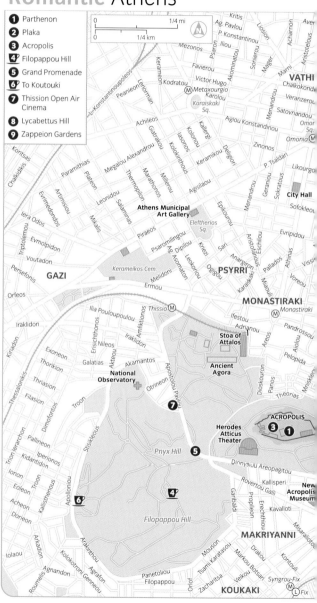

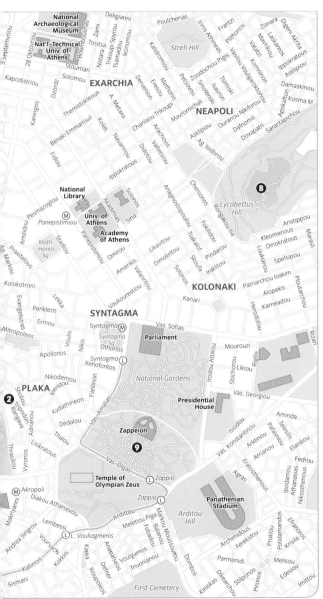

A thens has become a weekend destination in Europe, thanks to an influx of money from the 2004 Olympic Games, the sultry weather, and, of course, some of the most astonishing and important historic monuments in the world. It's true, many engaged couples or newlyweds only arrive en route to or from a Greek-island wedding, but with the surplus of outdoor cafes, boutiques, and sights, a romantic getaway in the city—with the Acropolis in the background—isn't so bad either! START: **Metro to Syntagma.**

1 ★★★ Parthenon. Anywhere with a view of the 156m (512-ft.) Sacred Rock—which is pretty much everywhere, since it towers some 70m (230 ft.) over the city—is going to be special. Be sure to take time out to catch a glimpse after the sun has gone down, when it is floodlit—a particularly good spot can be found from the infinity pool on the terrace of the King George Palace Hotel's penthouse suite, for a price. Fortunately, there are plenty of other restaurants and hotels to choose from to suit every budget. *Dionysiou Areopagitou St.*

2 ★★★ kids Plaka. Wander the whitewashed, island-village-like paths in **Anafiotika.** Then imagine yourself living in one of those beautifully restored 19th-century mansions around the east face of the Acropolis. This area, with its neoclassical buildings, is one of the most expensive, and it shows, but so does the charm. *See p 34,* **6**.

3 ★★★ kids Acropolis. This is the point, isn't it? *See p 9,* **3**.

4 ★ Filopappou Hill. If you're in Athens when the weather's comfortable (from late Mar to May and late Sept to Nov), make yourself a picnic lunch and head for the hill. Go toward **Agios Dimitrios** church (see p 45, **2**), a favorite for weddings, opposite the entrance to the Acropolis. Veer left/east on the trails up Filopappou Hill and find yourself a shady spot to clink glasses and Parthenon-gaze—a day you won't soon forget. *See p 83,* **3**.

5 ★★★ Grand Promenade. Walk along the cobblestone pedestrian roads that link up the ancient sites, from Parliament down through the shopping district (Ermou St.), to Kerameikos and Gazi, back to Thissio (Apostolou Pavlou St.) and around toward the Acropolis entrance (Dionysiou Areopagitou St.). In the evening you'll find couples sitting at various intervals along the low walls, together with the odd busker, and there are also benches in pleasant,

The old-world island charm of houses in the Plaka give the central city neighborhood the feel of a village.

Sunset at the cafe atop Lycabettus Hill, with the city laid out below, can be breathtaking.

secluded spots. The Sanctuary of the Nymph, where brides-to-be in antiquity made offerings for a happy marriage, is located near the Herodes Atticus Theater and the entrance to the Acropolis. *See p 9,* **2**.

6 **To Koutouki.** For a really rustic Greek experience, climb up the steep steps to the roof of this grill taverna on **Pnyx Hill,** where the waiters ream off a list of specialties for the day, from hot and cold salads and dips to lamb (by the kilo), pork, or steak specialties. Order the house wine, sit back, catch the breeze, and glance over at the Parthenon, getting an unusual and beautiful west-facing view. Dinner hour is 10pm, so be there an hour before or after to get a terrace table. *9 Lykeio St. at Agia Sotira church on Filopappou ring road.* ☎ *210/345-3655. Daily 7pm–2am. No credit cards. $$.*

7 **★★★ Thission Open-Air Cinema.** Watch a classic or memory-making first-run film (don't worry—they're subtitled) under the stars in a garden setting, then head to a very contemporary cafe-bar on the square. This small outdoor theater is like a time warp to the 1950s. *See p 121.*

8 **★ Lycabettus Hill.** Everything is romantic from on high, so make your way up the 277m (909-ft.) hill for the best panoramic view of the city during the day or at night, and have a drink or coffee. (You can huff and puff it up the trail, or take the cog railway.) The Mediterranean-cuisine-serving **cafe** at the top is cheaper than the restaurant, but still captive-market pricey. *See p 35,* **9**.

9 **Zappeion Gardens.** This oasis of the city is adjacent to the National Gardens, originally the private garden of Greece's first queen, Amalia. It's perfect for a refreshing

A statue of a nymph in the Zappeion Gardens, actually a continuation of the National Gardens.

A Spa Experience

For lovers who'd rather relax, there is an award-winning luxury spa right in the center of town: The **Grande Bretagne Hotel Spa ★★★** in Syntagma Square (☎ 210/333-0799; www.grandebretagne.gr) will give both of you face or body treatments, followed by side-by-side massages, though there is a range of other options, from a quickie express massage to half-day and full-day wedding packages. They also have an indoor pool with hydrojets, a sauna, and various steam rooms. Or go next door, where you can spend all day luxuriating in the indoor pool, Jacuzzi, or sauna at the **King George Palace Hotel Spa,** 3 Vas. Georgiou St. (☎ 210/322-2210; www.classicalhotels.com), for only 20€. They also have various beauty treatments and massages, while in the off season you can go upstairs to the Tudar Hall restaurant and have a mid-afternoon, Acropolis-view coffee. For a quick stop, the aptly named **Quick Spa,** 50–52 Aiolou and 31 Miltiadou sts. (☎ 210/325-5545; www.quickspa.gr), is centrally located and offers Shiatsu massages, facials, manicures, and pedicures for him and her at nondeluxe prices.

break in the hot summer months. It doesn't close, so if you end up here for some predawn smooching, you might find yourself in the company of fellow trysters (of the same gender by reputation). If you're just in the mood for a coffee, **Aigli,** the very chic, very pricey bistro in the gardens, has a cafe, so you can sip one at your lounge-y table inside or outside on the veranda. See p 21, ❽. ●

The Grande Bretagne Spa has an indoor pool with hydrojets, as well as a traditional sauna, steam baths, and a fully equipped fitness center.

Ancient Athens

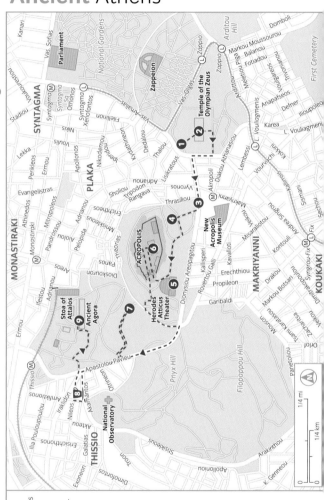

1. Hadrian's Arch
2. Temple of Olympian Zeus
3. Grand Promenade
4. Theater of Dionysos
5. Herodes Atticus Theater
6. Parthenon
7. Aeropagus
8. Skales
9. Ancient Agora

Previous Page: An old doorway typical of the island-village-like neighborhood of Plaka.

A thenians are reaping the rewards of a 40-million-euro urban renewal and archaeological site reunification project implemented in 2004. It's a revised version of an 1832 plan by Greek and Bavarian architects who laid out the then-fledgling modern Greek capital. The project links up the ancient sites, monuments, green areas, and squares in Athens's historic center along a pedestrian walkway that roughly corresponds to ancient pathways. Building facades were also restored and billboards removed. The change, aesthetically and in quality of life, has been nothing short of stellar.

START: **Metro to Akropoli.**

1 Hadrian's Arch. Start a tour from this photogenic 2nd-century gate built for Emperor Hadrian, who expanded the city beyond the then-centuries-old Themistoclean Wall. He went through it en route to the newly completed Temple of Olympian Zeus. *See p 11,* **5**.

2 Temple of Olympian Zeus. Construction on this giant temple to the top god began with the tyrant Peisistratos in the mid-500s, and then stopped and started a few times during its 650-year building schedule as commissioners came and went. The stockpiled building materials were used elsewhere (in the Themistoclean Wall and the Capitoline Temple in Rome, for example). The 4,785-sq.-m (51,500-sq.-ft.) temple was finally completed by Hadrian, who put a copy of one of the seven wonders of the ancient world, Pheidias's statue of Zeus, inside it, plus one of himself. It's located at an ancient outdoor sanctuary dedicated to Zeus, and the columns alone tower at 17m (56 ft.) high. *See p 22,* **10**.

3 ★★★ Grand Promenade. Start walking up pedestrian Dionysiou Areopagitou Street, along this walkway around the Acropolis. Note the marble-and-statue-facade Art

Hadrian's Arch, adjacent to the busy Amalias Avenue, is constructed entirely of Pentelic marble.

Deco buildings just past the New Acropolis Museum on your left—at the time of publication, protesters were petitioning to save them from demolition for obstructing the museum's view. See p 9, ②.

④ **Theater of Dionysos.** The first and oldest theater in Athens, dating to the 6th century B.C., this is where the Assembly met (after they moved off Pnyx Hill, in the 3rd c. B.C., perhaps due to the distractingly beautiful view of the Parthenon) and where competitions took place for the best dramas in honor of the pleasure god, Dionysos. It held some 17,000 spectators over its 750 years of reconstructions. Plays by Aeschylus, Aristophanes, Sophocles, and Euripides were performed here in classical times; gladiators and mock sea battles took place in Roman times. Also on the site are the **Panagia Chrysopolitissa** church; the ruins of the 5th-century-B.C. **Pericles Odeon** (used for musical performances); the **Asklepion,** a sanctuary and clinic dedicated to the god of medicine; and the 2nd-century-B.C. **Stoa of Eumenes,** a (then) covered walkway to the nearby **Herodes Atticus Theater,** built by the Pergamene king Eumenes II (198–159 B.C.), which you can still walk along en route to the **Acropolis.** 🕐 1 hr. Thrassilou & Dionysiou Areopagitou sts. ☎ 210/322-4625. www.culture.gr. Admission 2€ or part of Acropolis ticket. Daily Apr–Oct 8am–7:30pm; Nov–Mar 8am–5pm. Metro: Akropoli.

⑤ ★★★ **Herodes Atticus Theater.** Built by Athens benefactor Herodes Atticus in honor of his wife, Regilla, in the 2nd century A.D., the once cedar-roofed odeon at the foot of the Acropolis holds Athens Festival performances on balmy evenings. The marble seating dates from the 1950s, and popular performances are a squeeze for 5,000, but the ambiance is worth it. See p 122.

⑥ ★★★ **Parthenon.** This beautiful structure at the Acropolis may be for-

The audience seating areas and the stage of the 161 A.D. Herodes Atticus Theater were restored using marble in the 1950s.

The old-world allure of Skales, a Thissio cafe and meze (appetizer) restaurant.

8 **Skales.** Sit down for a coffee at an outdoor cafe on Thissio Square, or get something stronger across the street to go with a filling plate of *pikilia* (hot or cold mixed appetizers) at Skales (pronounced *ska*-less, "steps"), a *meze* restaurant next to the stairs between Nileos and Akamandos streets. *1 Nileos St.* ☎ *210/346-5647. $$.*

9 ★ **kids** **Ancient Agora.** Walk across the street through Thissio Square to one of the entrances of the Agora and see the Thisseion (also called the **Hephaisteion,** for Hephaestos, god of metalwork) temple up close, where philhellenic Protestants who fought during the War of Independence were buried. Then wander through the rest of the site to the re-created **Stoa of Attalos,** which now houses the Ancient Agora Museum, a gift of the Rockefellers. *See p 20,* **3**.

A headless statue of the Roman emperor and philosopher Hadrian (76–138 A.D.) looks onto the Ancient Agora's Hephaisteion.

ever under scaffolding, but it doesn't matter. Walk around, admire the view, and soak up the atmosphere, but do not pick up any (potentially ancient marble) pebbles. Lots of security is there to make sure you leave things as you found them at the site of Greece's most iconic national treasure. *See p 10,* **3**.

7 ★ **Areopagus.** Continue on your way around the pedestrian walkway, now called Apostolou Pavlou ("Apostle Paul's"). Opposite the Thission cinema is an entrance to Areopagus ("Ares Hill"), where trials were held in classical times. Ares himself was tried here by the pantheon of gods for the murder of Poseidon's son, according to myth. The apostle Paul preached here much later, in A.D. 51, which is noted on an embedded tablet opposite the entrance to the Acropolis. On this side of the hill, a bucolic path goes alongside the Ancient Agora to Plaka. ⏱ *20 min. Continuation of Theorias St. opposite Acropolis entrance. Metro: Akropoli or bus: 230.*

Syntagma to Gazi

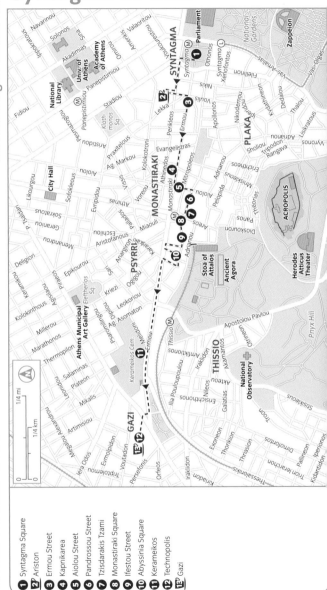

Y ou'll be in plenty of company on this walk, as it follows
the main shopping thoroughfare along Ermou, where you can
find a great pair of shoes. Then veer into Monastiraki to get your
souvenirs, see some sites, and admire the Acropolis view at a cafe.
Start in Syntagma Square, the main hub of Athens; then continue
west down Ermou Street and through Monastiraki, characterized by
cafes and a flea market that operates every day; pass Psyrri to the
north, where traditional-trade tinsmiths and tanneries are being fast
replaced by cafes, bars, and restaurants; and finally end your walk
in Gazi, named after the gasworks plant that dominates the area,
which has surged in popularity in the past few years. START: **Metro
to Syntagma.**

❶ Syntagma Square. Parliament faces the city's main square,
forming a point of the commercial
triangle (with Monastiraki and Omonia) in the historic center where you
can find major banks, travel agencies, and hotels. The 1830s-era
square has three parts: the Tomb
of the Unknown Soldier, the Metro
exit, and the top of Ermou Street. It
has hosted massive protest rallies,
New Year's celebrations, and major
historic events in the life of the
country, starting with its namesake:
The *syntagma* (constitution) was
demanded by the people from the
foot-dragging Bavarian King Otto
(installed by the Great Powers—the
United Kingdom, France, and the
Russian Empire—following the War
of Independence) in 1843. This is a
good place to stop for a rest or to
check your guidebook at a bench or
cafe near the central fountain. ⏱ *20
min. Amalias & Vas. Georgiou sts.
Metro: Syntagma.*

❷ Ariston. It's perfectly accept-
able to eat crumbly pies while on
the go. You can get your daily veg
cheaply at one of the oldest pita
bakeries, which makes vegetable-
and-meat-pie combinations such as
chicken, leek, and eggplant for
1.70€. Takeout only. *10 Voulis St.*
☎ *210/322-7626. $*

Evzones *(elite soldiers) guard the Tomb
of the Unknown Soldier in Syntagma
Square, as well as the Presidential Mansion and the Presidential Guard training
camp.*

❸ ★★★ Ermou Street. A busy
commercial street since the 19th
century, it was pedestrianized in the
1990s to misguided shopkeepers'
protests, who thought they'd lose
business. Do your shoe shopping
here. *See p 12,* ❽.

❹ ★ Kapnikarea. This charming
church has typical Athenian-style
domes and dates to 1050. While
dedicated to the Virgin Mary, it has

Shoppers on Ermou Street, the central commercial avenue of Athens, may find clothes, cosmetics, bags, books, and especially shoes there.

been called various names over the years, but the one that stuck likely refers to a Byzantine-era tax or to the surname of the church's sponsor. *See p 46,* **4**.

5 ★ **Aiolou Street.** Veer left for 2 blocks on the circa-1835 street named for Aeolus, god of wind, which leads to . . . the **Tower of the Winds.** But don't follow the road all the way to the tower—turn left before you reach it, so you can enjoy Pandrossou Street. *See p 12,* **10**.

6 **Pandrossou Street.** This pedestrian alley was the Turkish bazaar, one of the last vestiges of 400 years of Ottoman rule that ended in the 1820s. No longer the

The Millennium Globe, *a sculpture symbolizing world peace, rests at the center of the Technopolis grounds.*

flea market, as the banner over the street at Mitropoleos Square suggests, it has long gone upmarket with souvenir and jewelry shops. *Pandrossou St. at Mitropoleos Sq.*

7 **Tzisdarakis Tzami.** The Turkish *viovode* (governor) felled an Olympian Zeus temple column to plaster his namesake mosque in 1759. The remaining columns are said to have noisily mourned their sister's loss until the governor, exiled by his superior for the vandalism, was killed. It was used as a prison before being converted to a museum in 1918, now the Ceramic Folk Art Museum. *See p 26,* **1**.

8 ★★ **Monastiraki Square.** The congested square in front of Monastiraki Station is named for the **Little Monastery,** a badly restored 10th-to-17th-century church that belonged to a Greek Orthodox convent. It's forever behind barriers, as the square keeps getting remodeled—hence the congestion. Have a coffee or souvlaki at one of the cafe-restaurants here, or around the corner on **Adrianou Street,** where you'll also get an Acropolis view over the Ancient Agora. *Ermou & Athinas sts.*

9 **Ifestou Street.** This alley is full of shops catering to youths (beads, boots, shirts), tourists (souvenirs, jewelry), and antique/flea-market lovers (miscellaneous junk), plus the odd shop thrown in, like one that sells bicycles. *Ifestou St. at Monastiraki Sq.*

10 ★ **Abyssinia Square.** This name may refer to Ethiopians who lived here, but the square is also known as Paliatzidika (the "second-hand-shop district"), as this is where a flea market and a few household-goods auctions (on Sun) are located. *Ermou, Normanou & Kinetou sts.*

11 **Kerameikos.** Located in what was the pottery district of classical

Agia Triada, a Byzantine church on the grounds of the Kerameikos cemetery, is dedicated to the Holy Trinity.

known sites in Athens but is beautiful nonetheless: Despite the busy location, it's peaceful to meander among the monuments. The museum is remarkable, too. ⏱ *1 hr. 148 Ermou St.* ☎ *210/346-3552. Part of the 12€ Acropolis ticket package. Museum & site 2€. Mon–Sun 8am–7:30pm. Metro: Thissio.*

Athens, this ancient cemetery has burial artifacts dating from the 11th century B.C. to the 2nd century A.D. It also contains ruins of the 5th-century-B.C. "Long Walls," which provided a corridor from Athens to the sea outlet of Piraeus, and the Dipylon Gate (the main entrance to ancient Athens). Sections of Iera Odos (the "Sacred Way"), an important road that lead from Athens to Demeter's temple in ancient Eleusis, now modern Elefsina (22km/14 miles away), are also here. Kerameikos is one of the lesser

⑫ ★★ Technopolis. Industrial-design and *Metropolis* film lovers will adore this unique converted gasworks. Dating from 1862, with additions in 1896 and the mid-1900s, it fueled the city's network of lights with gas. The site and its unusual mix of buildings are now used to host concerts and exhibitions, as well as the City of Athens radio station. There's a cafe on-site. At night, the smokestacks are lit up as if red hot. *See p 13,* **⑭**.

⑬ ★ Gazi. Go inside the **Technopolis** complex, the old gasworks, where there's a **cafe** (☎ 210/347-0981) in one of the buildings on the grounds. If it isn't open, you can stop for coffee or a meal at the many places along Persefonis Street, toward the Kerameikos Metro Station, that have opened up in this latest trendy area. *See p 13,* **⑭**.

Markets, shops, and crowds on the small Pandrossou Street in Monastiraki.

Plaka, Thissio & Psyrri

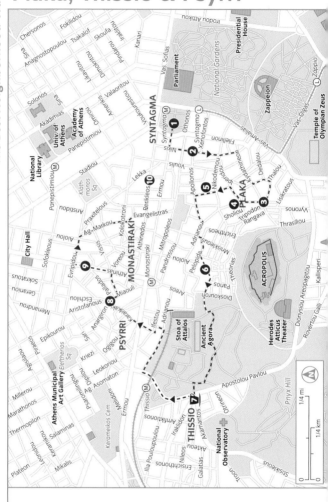

1. Syntagma Square
2. Nikis Street
3. Plaka
4. Adrianou Street
5. Hill Memorial School
6. Roman Agora
7. Thissio
8. Psyrri
9. Athinas Street
10. Perikleous Street

xperience a slice of Athens life by wandering through those districts where the locals shop; the whole area reaffirms that expertise-driven, mom-and-pop shops can thrive in mixed zoning—with Sundays off. Start in the historic Plaka zone, with its stately 19th-century buildings and tourist stores, then head through ancient parks into the cafe-lined streets of Thissio with its superlative Acropolis views. Turn northeast into hardware-heavy Athinas Street and the streets leading off it, through Psyrri and back eastward up to where you started. START: **Metro to Syntagma.**

A hand-painted doorway of a kafeneio (cafe) in Plaka is emblazoned with the current and past Greek flag.

1 Syntagma Square. Central Syntagma, the main square in town in front of Parliament, is the heart from which the arterial avenues of Athens lead off. This should be your starting point. *See p 59,* **1**.

2 Nikis Street. The first cross street west of Syntagma and often confused with Voulis Street (the next one down), Nikis is getting trendier by the day. It leads into Kydathineon Street, named after the ancient municipality, in Plaka. *Nikis & Ermou sts.*

3 ★★★ kids Plaka. This is the oldest (and most expensive) part of town hugging the north and east slopes of the Acropolis, there are both ruins and historic buildings to gawp at here, including the beautiful and unusual **Lysicrates** monument. Built to display tripod-braced trophies for the best play productions at the Dionysos Theater around the corner, it's named after the 334 B.C. winner. Ancient Tripodon Street, which still exists, was lined with similar monuments. Walk straight up Kydathineon Street to reach the island-style **Anafiotika** district. The area was settled by Cycladic island migrants, especially from the island of Anafi, who came to build the modern capital in the mid-1800s. *See p 34,* **6**.

4 Adrianou Street. This is the main street in Plaka, the long-inhabited area north of the Acropolis. It's lined with attractive 19th-century buildings with ground-floor tourist shops. Likely the city's oldest mansion (from the 17th or 18th c.) is in ruins behind the wall at no. 96, at the top of Palaiologou Venizelou Street, named for its owner (a magistrate). *Adrianou & Palaiologou Venizelou sts.*

5 Hill Memorial School. American John Henry Hill (1791–1882) opened a school for underprivileged girls here in 1831, receiving many awards for the effort, which lasted until 1982, when his descendants finally closed it. *9 Thoukididou St.*

A sidewalk cafe in front of ruins of the Roman Agora, which was a commercial hub from the 1st century B.C. to the 4th century A.D.

6 Roman Agora. The "new" Roman Agora was funded and built by Julius Caesar in 51 B.C. (and finished by Octavian Augustus in 19 B.C.), after wealthy, Athens-loving Romans had moved into the Ancient Agora site and built larger edifices there, thus crowding out merchants. It was larger than what we see now (much of it is now buried under buildings). The main remains most visible are the Tower of the Winds and the gate entrance to the market dedicated to Athena Archegetis ("Athena the Leader"), circa 11 B.C. The forlorn but beautiful Fetiye mosque on the site was built in 1458. *See p 12,* **10**.

7 ★★★ Thissio. Follow the top (south) boundary of the Roman Agora westward on Polygnotou Street (where the graffiti shows real talent) until you come to the Ancient Agora entrance. There's a lovely green area here where you can explore the north slope of the Acropolis. Continue on the **path** past the fenced-off Agii Apostoli church till you reach Thissio. Turn right (north), stop at one of the many outdoor **cafes** for refreshment, and marvel at the million-dollar view of both the Acropolis and Lycabettus Hill. *See p 9,* **1**.

A flower shop on a side street in fashionable Psyrri.

Psyrri's Charms

Psyrri offers the perfect showcase for a typical Athenian night out. A busy working neighborhood by day, the area is a magnet for nightlife-loving Athenians, and a stroll through the narrow pedestrian streets full of people on a cool evening always reaffirms my luck in actually living here. Patrons sit at tables lining the sidewalks around the squares, interrupted by the odd car trying to gain passage, a Roma child selling flowers, or an accordion troupe making its way from table to table. A mix of Greek restaurants, cafes, alternative bars and clubs, art galleries, theaters, and shops, Psyrri is Athens's prime entertainment zone.

8 ★★★ Psyrri. Continue into Psyrri, where you can stroll through the narrow streets interspersed with traditional small manufacturers, mostly leather-goods makers specializing in bags and shoes, tinsmiths, and basket weavers. At night, the area gets a second life when restaurants, bars, and clubs open. In 1809, poet and Greek War of Independence fighter Lord Byron boarded at 11 Agias Theklas St. (now a nondescript warehouse). He romanticized the owner's 12-year-old daughter, Teresa Makris, in "Maid of Athens." *See p 13, 12.*

9 ★ Athinas Street. Get a feel for the "handyman" part of town on Athinas Street, which anchors shops selling tools, votive candles, clothes, sandals, live chickens. . . . It leads to the **Central Market** (selling meat, fish, veggies, nuts, and so on). Veer right from Evripidou (Euripides) Street onto **Polykleitou,** which has some more interesting, real-deal shops, such as ones that sell only string, rope, and twine. *Athinas St. at Evripidou or Sofokleous sts.*

10 Perikleous Street. Make your way across to the relatively unglamorous Perikleous, one street north

and parallel to central Ermou Street, which changes names four times before reaching Athinas Street. Unlike Ermou's chain stores, here there are interesting things for sale, including ethnic items and polished stones—you can create your own earrings, necklaces, or bracelets with the trinkets found here. Follow Perikleous up (east), and you're back at central Syntagma Square. *Perikleous & Evangelistrias sts.*

Traditional briki (Greek coffee pots), like these for sale on Perikleous Street, allow for the proper amount of foam in your Greek coffee.

Kolonaki & Lycabettus

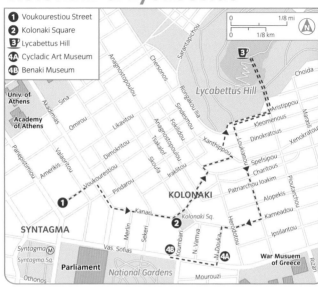

1 Voukourestiou Street
2 Kolonaki Square
3 Lycabettus Hill
4A Cycladic Art Museum
4B Benaki Museum

The perfectly coiffed, shod, and clothed can be found in Kolonaki. It's full of old-fashioned coffee bars that are proud to stay that way, chic designer shops, pedestrian streets, expensive whole-floor apartments, and people from Athens's upper echelons who aim to impress. START: **Metro to Syntagma.**

1 **Voukourestiou Street.** It has the most exclusive shops (Tod's shoes and Baccarat crystal, to name two), and streets that lead off it are lined with outdoor cafes (turn right on Skoufa or Tsakalof sts.). *Voukourestiou & Skoufa sts.*

2 ★ **Kolonaki Square.** Named for a remnant of a small column (*kolonaki*) in the middle of the square, it's officially called Filikis Etairias ("Friendly Society"). See and be seen at one of its outdoor cafes. *See p 17,* 5.

3 ★ **Lycabettus Hill.** Come up here for the sunset view over this city of four million and the island of

Aegina offshore as you sip your beverage of choice from the (pricey) **cafe.** See p 35, 9.

4A ★ **Cycladic Art** or 4B ★ **Benaki museums.** If it's not too late in the day, step from the heady Lycabettus and Kolonaki atmosphere into a private museum in one of the stately mansions just down from Kolonaki Square. The Cycladic Art Museum contains mostly that civilization's modern-looking sculptures, while the Benaki's collection ranges from antiquity to the 20th century. *See p 28 and 29,* 14 *or* 16. ●

Shopping **Best Bets**

A print of the Temple of Olympian Zeus from the aptly named Old Prints, Maps & Books.

Best **Folk Art**
★ Amorgos, *3 Kodrou St.*
(p 76)

Best **Original Art**
Astrolavos-Dexameni,
11 Xanthippou St. (p 71)

Best **Spice & Herb Shop**
★ Bahar, *31 Evripidou St. (p 75)*

Best **Museum Reproduction
Gifts**
★ Benaki Museum Gift Shop,
1 Koumbari St. (p 76)

Best **Bookstore**
Eleftheroudakis, *17 Panepistimiou St.*
(p 73)

Best **Sunday Flea Market**
★★ Gazi Flea Market, *Ermou &
Pareos sts. (p 79)*

Best **Traditional Greek Textiles**
★ ISPS Arts & Crafts, *14 Filellinon St.*
(p 77)

Best Place for **Designer Shoes**
Kalogirou, *4 Patriarchou Ioakim St.*
(p 80)

Best **Magazine Shop**
★★ Kiosk, *18 Omonia Sq.*
(p 73)

Best **Selection of Silverware**
Konstantopoulou, *23 Lekka St.*
(p 77)

Best Place for **Skincare
Products**
Korres, *8 Ivikou St. (p 72)*

Best Known **Athenian Jeweler**
★ Lalaounis, *6 Panepistimiou St.*
(p 78)

Best Place for **Traditional
Greek Coffees**
Loumidis, *106 Aiolou St. (p 76)*

Best Place for **Worry Beads**
★ Mala (Komboloi Club),
1 Praxitelous St. (p 77)

Best **Children's Shoes**
Mouyer, *6 Ermou St. (p 79)*

Best Place for **Locally Made
Shoes**
★★ Old Athens, *17 Kanari St. (p 80)*

Best Place for **Musical
Instruments**
Philippos Nakas Conservatory,
44 Panepistimiou St. (p 79)

Best **One-Stop Shop**
★★★ Shopping Center Plaka,
1 Pandrossou St. (p 78)

Previous page: A selection of ceramic chalices at the Sunday flea market in Monastiraki.

Monastiraki, Plaka & Omonia Shopping

Syntagma & Kolonaki Shopping

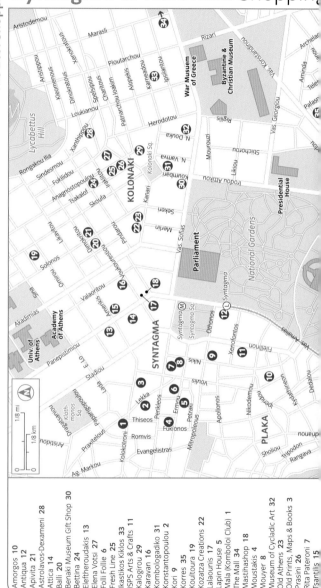

Athens Shopping A to Z

Antique guns, first-edition books, and prints for sale at Antiqua, which also sells old coins, swords, icons, and so on.

Antiques & Collectibles

Antiqua SYNTAGMA   Buy museum pieces such as 19th-century water-colors, pistols, and enormous belt buckles at this high-end antiques store that carries both Greek and foreign furniture and objets d'art. *2 Amalias Ave. ☎ 210/323-2220. www.antiqua.gr. AE, DC, MC, V. Metro: Syntagma. Map p 70.*

Old Prints, Maps & Books

SYNTAGMA   A handful of shops sell gravures of Athens and Greece, but this one also carries old maps, books, and drawings of "other romantic subjects" such as birds and plants, from 20€ without frame. *15 Kolokotroni St. ☎ 210/323-0923. Fax 210/323-0788. www.oldprints.gr. AE, DC, MC, V. Metro: Syntagma or bus: 200. Map p 70.*

Art

Astrolavos-Dexameni KOLONAKI Take home a painting by a well-known Greek artist or a conversation piece by an up-and-coming one from this gallery, which has another branch in

Kolonaki, at 11 Irodotou St. (☎ 210/722-1200), as well as in Piraeus, at 140 Androutsou St. (☎ 210/412-8002). *11 Xanthippou St. ☎ 210/729-4342 or 210/729-4343. www.astrolavos.gr. AE, DC, MC, V. Metro: Syntagma. Map p 70.*

Papier-mâché work by Artemis Makridou, from Astrolavos-Dexameni.

Handmade-in-Greece body oils and creams on the shelves at Fresh Line.

Ekklesiastika Eidi MONASTIRAKI
This shop may be out of the ecclesiastical-accouterments neighborhood (Apollonos St.) but is conveniently located near Agia Eirini church, advertises "unbeatable prices" on church supplies, and has a large showroom and workshop on the premises to make any saint's icons you like, in silver, wood, and so on. *9 Agias Eirinis St.* ☎ *210/325-2047. AE, DC, V. Metro: Monastiraki. Map p 69.*

Ikastikos Kiklos KOLONAKI
A big gallery, it exhibits most contemporary Greek artists. The main location is at 121 Harilaou Trikoupi St. (☎ 210/330-0136). See items for sale online under "Gallery." *20 Karneadou St.* ☎ *210/729-1642. www.ikastikos-kiklos.gr. AE, MC, V. Metro: Syntagma. Map p 70.*

Beauty & Toiletries
Apivita KOLONAKI   Those hooked on Propoline hair care (made from bee products) might be able to find it at home, since this popular maker of natural beauty products is available in 16 countries. In Greece the brand is carried in most pharmacies.

26 Solonos St. ☎ *210/364-0560. www.apivita.com. MC, V. Metro: Panepistimiou or bus: A5, E7, 060, 224. Map p 70.*

Fresh Line KOLONAKI   On display, beauty products and pyramids of colorful rough-cut soaps containing rice, seaweed, honey, and other all-natural organically grown ingredients look good enough to eat. *10 Skoufa St.* ☎ *210/364-4015. www.freshline.gr. AE, MC, V. Metro: Syntagma. Map p 70.*

Hondos Center OMONIA   The flagship store of this toiletries chain has all the grooming items you'll ever need, with lavish perfume counters, complete product lines, accessories, and even luggage. Come here when you need to restock or get sunscreen, then go to the top floor and enjoy the view of the city over coffee. *4 Omonia Sq.* ☎ *210/528-2800. www.hondos.gr. AE, DC, MC, V. Metro: Omonia. Map p 69.*

Korres PANGRATI   This purse-, flora-, and fauna-friendly skin-care line by an herbal pharmacist is used by the likes of the Beckhams. It's

The skin-care product line by Korres is on display at its headquarters in Athens and is sold around the world.

Where to Get It

Jewelry, shoes, and edibles are standouts in Greece. For hip and **cool,** head to the streets around youth-zone Exarchia Square, or Ifestou Street in Monastiraki. Kolonaki is the **upmarket designer** district, while **shoes** and **chain stores** are on central Ermou Street. **Souvenirs** and **jewelry** are mainly on Adrianou Street in Plaka, down to Pandrossou Street in Monastiraki. For **made-in-Greece goods** go to the streets leading off Athinas. Running from Athinas toward Stadiou Street are shops grouped together by merchandise, such as **textiles** (Athinaidos St.) and **church-related supplies** (Apollonos St., near the Mitropoleos cathedral). Abyssinia Square in Monastiraki is a **flea market** that also sells **used and antique furniture.** Be wary that Athens street names may change depending on the area or block (Adrianou, for example) and the Latin spelling, so keep a good map at hand.

available at most pharmacies and the Attica Department Store, as well as at the flagship store in Pangrati. *8 Ivikou St. at Erathosthenous St.* ☎ *210/722-2774. www.korres.com. AE, DC, MC, V. Metro: Syntagma. Map p 70.*

Books & Magazines
Eleftheroudakis SYNTAGMA
Find English titles on any subject in the eight-story Panepistimiou location that has a whole floor devoted to travel books, as well as a cafe-restaurant to rest at after hours of browsing. *17 Panepistimiou St.* ☎ *210/325-8440. www.books.gr. AE, DC, MC, V. Metro: Panepistimiou. Map p 70.*

★★ **Kiosk** OMONIA SQUARE
Athens's best-stocked foreign-press *periptero* (kiosk) never closes, which is fortunate for desperate or jet-lagged news and magazine junkies. My favorite place to buy obscure magazines. *18 Omonia Sq. at Athinas St., in front of Everest (fast food).* ☎ *210/322-2402. No credit cards. Metro: Omonia. Map p 69.*

Koultoura ACADEMIAS/KOLONAKI
This unmarked basement store on a blink-and-miss pedestrian walkway has rare Greek and foreign books. *4 Mantzarou St. between Sina & Omirou sts.* ☎ *210/363-6281. No credit cards. Metro: Panepistimiou or bus: A5, E7, 060, 224. Map p 70.*

Kiosk's multitude of Greek and foreign-press magazines and newspapers.

Cigars
Balli KOLONAKI   As to be expected in Kolonaki, this is a high-end emporium that stocks all (and only) Cuban cigars and smoking-related accessories. *25 Voukourestiou St.* ☎ *210/360-8425. www.balli.com.gr. AE, MC, V. Metro: Syntagma. Map p 70.*

Costumes
Igglesi MITROPOLEOS   For Carnival, Halloween, and even ancestral costumes, including the pleated *foustanella* skirt for men, from any domestic or diaspora region, head to this little shop. *6 Venizelou St. at Mitropoleos Sq.* ☎ *210/322-1261. MC, V. Metro: Monastiraki or Syntagma or bus: 025, 026, 027. Map p 69.*

Department Stores
Attica SYNTAGMA   This institution has all sorts of goods—if you want to check out or purchase up-and-coming Greek designers, you can find Eleftheriadis (Collage Sociale), Erotokritos (Eros), and Celia Kritharioti (5226 by Celia Kritharioti) in the

Dresses on sale at the boutique Bettina, which offers fashion from international designers.

eight-floor "shop-in-shop." It's best to buy in August and January when the sales are on. *9 Panepistimiou St.* ☎ *211/180-2600. www.atticadps.gr. AE, DC, MC, V. Metro: Syntagma. Map p 70.*

F-Fokas PANEPISTIMIOU   Another shop-in-shop for clothes, this time more brand-name sports- and casual wear, including for children. *41 Stadiou St.* ☎ *210/325-7770. www.fokas.gr. AE, DC, MC, V. Metro: Syntagma. Map p 69.*

The Mall MAROUSSI   For those who must go to one, Greece's largest mall was built here in 2005, by one of the shipping dynasties (Latsis). It has four levels, some 200 shops, a food court, an entertainment complex, and a convenient Metro station entrance. *35 Andrea Papandreou St.* ☎ *210/630-0000. www.themallathens.gr. Metro or Proastiakos: Nerantziotissa.*

Notos Home OMONIA   Notos has nice home accessories small enough to carry, especially on the ground level. There's also a trendy restaurant on the eighth floor. If you're looking for clothes and perfume, head to their store at 99 Aiolou St. (☎ 210/324-5811). *5 Kratinou St. at Kotzia Sq.* ☎ *210/374-3000. www.notos home.gr. AE, DC, MC, V. Metro: Omonia. Map p 69.*

Fashion
Bettina KOLONAKI   Well-known Greek designer Angelos Frentzos shares rack space with international labels at this boutique. *40 Pindarou & 29 Anagnostopoulou sts.* ☎ *210/339-2094. AE, DC, MC, V. Metro: Syntagma or bus: 200. Map p 70.*

★ **Kourbela** PLAKA   Comfy, reasonably priced, and eco-friendly linen-and-silk-and-cotton-blend unisex clothing (from the "Earth Collection") is sold at this corner shop (no

St. ☎ 210/322-7101. www.rita paateroni.gr. DC, MC, V. Metro: Syntagma. Map p 70.

Tsantilis SYNTAGMA This shop has various branches around town that also sell material. It's well-known for stocking good-quality fabrics and designer clothing at reasonable prices. 6 Panepistimiou St. at Voukourestiou St. ☎ 210/360-6815. www.tsantilis.gr. DC, MC, V. Metro: Syntagma. Map p 70.

Food & Wine

★ **Bahar** AGORA Take home big bags of oregano, mountain tea, and many more obscure herbs that also make welcome (and cheap) gifts—and can easily pass customs. 31 Evripidou St. ☎ 210/321-7225. www.bahar-spices.gr. No credit cards. Metro: Omonia or Monastiraki or bus: 025, 026, 027, 035, 049, 200, 227. Map p 69.

A combination from Rita Pateroni, who designs women's prêt-à-porter and tailor-made garments.

sign), alongside Greek-made classic knits. I can't get enough of them. 109 Adrianou St. ☎ 210/322-4591. AE, DC, MC, V. Metro: Syntagma or Monastiraki. Map p 69.

Rita Pateroni SYNTAGMA You can take home well-priced, pretty clothing by a Greek designer on this increasingly trendy street parallel to pricey Ermou. 11 Karagiorgi Servias

The Greek Shop PLAKA Traditional-Greek-products shops are springing up all over, and although most are overpriced and overpackaged, this one is well stocked and

Culinary herbs and spices in bags at Bahar, one of the many spice shops fronting Evripidou Street.

KPEMMYΔI FLAKES
80 € / KIΛO

Karavan's rows of chocolates are superbly delicious, but it's really known for its baklava.

convenient on the main Plaka street. *120 Adrianou St.* ☎ *210/322-6850. Fax 210/324-9543. AE, DC, MC, V. Metro: Syntagma. Map p 69.*

Karavan SYNTAGMA The gooey-dessert deprived can sate their cravings here, as this chain store is known for its bite-sized, honey-soaked baklava and *kadaifi* (Greek pastry with nuts and syrup). *11 Voukourestiou St.* ☎ *210/364-1540. www.karavan.gr. No credit cards. Metro: Syntagma. Map p 70.*

Loumidis OMONIA This old-fashioned coffee roaster has been around since 1920. Here you'll find Greek coffee and the *briki* (traditional little coffee pots) to make it with. *106 Aiolou St. at Panepistimiou St.* ☎ *210/321-6965. No credit cards. Metro: Omonia. Map p 69.*

Mastihashop SYNTAGMA All kinds of products are made from the island of Chios's unique, medicinal, and tasty mastic gum. Here they're packaged in attractive, old-fashioned tins. The *loukoumi* (Turkish Delight) is a standout. *Panepistimiou & Kriezotou sts.* ☎ *210/363-2750.*

www.mastihashop.gr. AE, MC, V. Metro: Syntagma. Map p 70.

Gifts

★ **Amorgos** PLAKA This store has an exhaustive choice of anything Greek-made, from wooden folk pieces whose use has long been forgotten to delicate embroideries and linens. *3 Kodrou St.* ☎ *210/324-3836. AE, DC, MC, V. Metro: Syntagma. Map p 70.*

★ **Benaki Museum Gift Shop** KOLONAKI The museum stocks a variety of exhibit reproductions of gold and silver jewelry, textiles, decorative child-sized chairs, and ceramic bowls, as well as a good selection of translated books on Greece. *1 Koumbari St. at Vas. Sofias Ave.* ☎ *210/ 367-1000. www.benaki.gr. AE, DC, MC, V. Map p 70.*

Center of Hellenic Tradition
MONASTIRAKI A good place to find genuine folk arts and crafts from around Greece, including pottery, decorative roof tiles, and old-fashioned painted-wood shop signs. *36 Pandrossou & 59 Mitropoleos sts.* ☎ *210/321-3023. AE, DC, MC, V. Metro: Monastiraki. Map p 69.*

★ **Ekavi** MONASTIRAKI Get hand-made *tavli* (backgammon) board games—the *kafeneion* (cafe) brigade's game of choice—or chess sets, with pieces resembling Olympic athletes, Greek gods, and so on, in wood, metal, or stone. *36 Mitropoleos St.* ☎ *210/323-7740. www.manopoulos.com. AE, DC, MC, V. Metro: Monastiraki or Syntagma or bus: 025, 026, 027. Map 69.*

Evrika PLAKA Pick up official Athens 2004 mementos, football (soccer) shirts, and other souvenirs from this ex–Olympic store outlet. *69 Adrianou St.* ☎ *210/325-1935. AE, DC, MC, V. Metro: Monastiraki or Syntagma. Map p 69.*

Backgammon or tavli boards, like these from Ekavi, are a common pastime in Greek cafes.

★ ISPS Arts & Crafts ZAPPEION
For traditional Greek designs made in Greece, come to this store. It sells rugs, tapestries, and beautifully embroidered linens that are made by disadvantaged women around the country. Prices start at 20€ for a small embroidery. *14 Filellinon St.* ☎ *210/325-0240. www.oikotexnia-ikpa.gr. AE, DC, MC, V. Metro: Syntagma. Map p 70.*

Kombologadiko KOLONAKI
Bone, stone, wood, and antique amber are used to make these globally sourced *komboloi* ("worry beads) at the "exclusive" branch of this store (don't even try to say the name). *6 Koumbari St.* ☎ *212/700-0090. www.kombologadiko.gr. AE, DC, MC, V. Metro: Syntagma. Map p 70.*

Konstantopoulou SYNTAGMA
A large silverware store among many along "Silver Alley," it sells bowls, candlesticks, lamps, cutlery, and the like. *23 Lekka St.* ☎ *210/322-7997. AE, DC, MC, V. Metro: Syntagma. Map p 70.*

Kori SYNTAGMA   An eclectic selection of artifacts, both traditional and contemporary, by up-and-coming and also more established Greek talents. *13 Mitropoleos St.* ☎ *210/323-3534. AE, DC, MC, V. Metro: Syntagma. Map p 70.*

★ Mala (Komboloi Club)
SYNTAGMA   For all kinds of beads, head to Praxitelous Street. This shop in particular specializes in beautiful amber worry beads that are also easy to take home. From 15€ to 9,000€. *1 Praxitelous St.* ☎ *210/331-0145. www.komboloiclub.com. MC, V. Metro: Panepistimiou. Map p 70.*

★ Museum of Cycladic Art
KOLONAKI   Get modernist Cycladic figurines, art posters, jewelry, and other reproductions from this

A selection of silverware from Konstantopoulou on Lekka Street, which has silver shops selling everything from candlesticks to jewelry.

museum's collection. *4 N. Douka St. at Vas. Sofias Ave.* ☎ *210/722-8321 or 210/722-8323. www.cycladic.gr. Closed Tues & Sun. AE, DC, MC, V. Metro: Syntagma. Map p 70.*

★★★ **Shopping Center Plaka** MONASTIRAKI Do all your souvenir shopping in one go at this super-stocked three-level store that straddles the Ermou, Plaka, and Monastiraki districts. Also one of the few places that stocks writing paper (and with a Greek motif). *1 Pandrossou St.* ☎ *210/324-5405. www.shoppingplaka.com. AE, MC, V. Metro: Monastiraki. Map p 69.*

Jewelry

Elena Votsi KOLONAKI Winner of the competition to redesign the Olympic medal for Athens 2004 and onward, Votsi's larger-than-life jewelry is as heavy as your neck, wrist, or finger can stand—and popular with statement-making celebs. *7 Xanthou St.* ☎ *210/360-0936. www.elenavotsi.com. Metro: Syntagma. Map p 70.*

Prewrapped boxes of boubouniera (gifts or favors for guests of a baptism) from Angela.

Folli Follie SYNTAGMA This chain seller of internationally appealing and trendy costume jewelry, watches, and accessories in gold and silver has outlets as far away as Tokyo and as near as the airport. *18 Ermou St.* ☎ *210/323-0729. www.follifollie.gr. AE, DC, MC, V. Metro: Syntagma. Map p 70.*

★ **Lalaounis** SYNTAGMA A luxury brand, Lalaounis is perhaps the best known among many superb jewelers for crafting ancient and Byzantine reproductions as well as modern creations. *6 Panepistimiou St. at Voukourestiou St.* ☎ *210/361-1371. Museum: 12 Karyatidon St., Makriyanni.* ☎ *210/922-1044. www.lalaounis-jewelrymuseum.gr. AE, DC, MC, V. Map p 70.*

Ruby's PLAKA Get good-quality, made-on-site (a rarity) jewelry that won't break the bank at this long-established shop. They can also make your own design, engrave, or change your ring size while you wait. *105 Adrianou St.* ☎ *210/322-3312. AE, DC, MC, V. Map p 69.*

Kids

kids Angela MONASTIRAKI Get traditional baptism or christening clothes and related items here, including *boubouniera* (unique baptism favors). *9 Kalamiotou St. at Kapnikareas St.* ☎ *210/323-8448. www.angela.gr. Metro: Monastiraki. Map p 69.*

kids Ea MONASTIRAKI Find whimsical piggy banks, fairies, dolls, and other toys, plus unique knickknacks and home decorations in this spacious shop on a street parallel to pricey Ermou. *9 Agia Irinis Sq. at Aiolou & Athinaidos sts.* ☎ *210/321-8562. DC, MC, V. Metro: Monastiraki. Map p 69.*

kids Lapin House SYNTAGMA
This Greek chain offers up really
nice, good-quality kid's clothes—but
with a price tag to match. *21 Ermou
St.* ☎ *210/324-1316. www.lapin
house.com. AE, DC, MC, V. Metro:
Syntagma. Map p 70.*

kids Mouyer
SYNTAGMA
This shop with
the distinctive
house-in-a-shoe
storefront sign has been
making sturdy children's shoes
since 1900. *6 Ermou St.* ☎ *210/323-
2831. www.mouyer.gr. AE, DC, MC,
V. Metro: Syntagma. Map p 70.*

*A girl's shoe from the esteemed (and
expensive) Greek brand name Mouyer.*

Markets

★★ Central Market OMONIA
This is one of the best things about
Athens. Farmers' markets appear
once a week in neighborhoods
around town, but the main one for
more than a century is the Varvakio
Agora—a visual, aural, and olfactory
slap. *Athinas St. at Sofokleous St.
Mon–Thurs 6am–3pm; Fri–Sat 6am–
6pm. Metro: Omonia or Monastiraki
or bus: 025, 026, 035, 049, 100, 200,
227, 400. Map p 69.*

★★ Gazi Flea Market GAZI
This is a real flea market, which has
shifted to the Kerameikos Park area
at the end of Ermou Street. It's
mostly junk, but you can score
some good finds on a fun outing,
such as a brass pestle and mortar
for half the price as at a shop in the
Monastiraki Flea Market. Watch your
wallet, though, as there are a lot of
people in close proximity here.
*Ermou & Piraeus sts. Sun early
morning to 3 or 4pm. Metro: Thissio
or Kerameikos. Map p 69.*

Monastiraki Flea Market

MONASTIRAKI In the narrow alleys
of the Monastiraki district, particularly along Pandrossou and Ifestou

streets, are myriad trinket and arti-
fact shops. The "official" flea market, though, has been held in
Abyssinia Square since 1910. You'll
find dusty books, military uniforms,
coins and stamps, light fixtures,
plates, cutlery, furniture—any sec-
ondhand estate contents, really.
*Abyssinia Sq. at Ermou, Nor-
manou & Kinetou sts.
Daily 9am–9pm; best
on Sun. Metro:
Monastiraki.
Map p 69.*

Music
Metropolis
OMONIA This
five-floor depart-
ment store of
music is the city's best known, and
also a concert and event ticket outlet.
Prolific Greek music is sold at the
no. 54 address, with its distinctive
wrought-iron overhang; no. 64 sells
both foreign and Greek titles. *54 & 64
Panepistimiou St.* ☎ *210/380-8549.
www.metropolis.gr. AE, DC, MC, V.
Metro: Omonia. Map p 69.*

Pegasus MONASTIRAKI Genuine
bouzouki instruments are handmade and sold from 150€ at this
shop, along with stringed *taboura*
(a type of lute) and small hand-held
"bongo" *touberlekia* drums. Get one
to play, hang, or prop against a wall.
26 Pandrossou St. ☎ *210/324-2036.
92 Adrianou St.* ☎ *210/324-2601.
www.pegasusgreece.com. AE, DC,
MC, V. Metro: Monastiraki. Map
p 69.*

**Philippos Nakas Conserva-
tory** OMONIA Buy an instrument,
music sheets, or related gadgets at
this serious chain of music stores, or
buy online from their catalog. *44
Panepistimiou St.* ☎ *210/361-2720.
www.nakas.gr. AE, DC, MC, V. Metro:
Panepistimiou. Map p 69.*

Musical instruments are sold at Philippos Nakas Conservatory, which is one of the leading music schools in Greece.

Shoes

Intersport Athletics OMONIA
If your hard-traveling trainers have packed up and gone, this shop on "Runner Alley" has about the best selection to get a new pair. There's a large branch near Monastiraki station, at 87–89 Ermou St. (☎ 210/321-1282), too. *3 Themistokleous St.* ☎ *210/330-3997. www.intersport.gr. AE, DC, MC, V. Metro: Omonia. Map p 69.*

Kalogirou KOLONAKI There's a large selection of designer shoes at this busy branch of a well-known, high-end shoe store. *4 Patriarchou Ioakim St.* ☎ *210/335-6401. www. lemonis.gr. AE, DC, MC, V. Metro: Syntagma or bus: 022, 060, 200. Map p 70.*

Kozatsa Creations KOLONAKI Get made-to-order leather shoes or

buy house styles for 130€ to 150€ (with pretty, nonteetering heels) before the shoemaker retires. *11 Kanari St.* ☎ *210/362-7592. No credit cards. Metro: Syntagma. Map p 70.*

Moustakis SYNTAGMA One among many on shoe lovers' Ermou Street, but this local shoemaker also does half-sizes—a rarity. *36 Ermou St.* ☎ *210/323-2641. DC, MC, V. Metro: Syntagma. Map p 70.*

★★ Old Athens KOLONAKI Get a pair of jaw-droppingly beautiful, classy, and chic shoes made in Greece from here. *17 Kanari St.* ☎ *210/361-4762. AE, DC, MC, V. Metro: Syntagma. Map p 70.*

Prasini KOLONAKI Fashionistas flock to this designer-shoe-selling shop that also sells brand-name bags. *7–9 Tsakalof St.* ☎ *210/364-6258. AE, DC, MC, V. Metro: Syntagma. Map p 70.*

Spiliopoulos MONASTIRAKI A vast (relatively speaking) array of designer shoes at bargain prices. They are "seconds" that never made it past quality control, but who could find the flaw? Be prepared to fight for bench space. Also stocked are bags, wallets, and purses. *63 Ermou St.* ☎ *210/322-7590. AE, MC, V. 50 Adrianou St.* ☎ *210/321-9096. DC, MC, V. Metro: Monastiraki. Map p 69.*

Stavros Melissinos PSYRRI This is where the distinctive leather sandal worn by the likes of Sophia Loren, Jackie O., and Anthony Quinn originated in 1954. The famed "poet shoemaker's" son, a costume designer and artist, now runs it. *2 Agias Theklas St.* ☎ *210/321-9247. www. melissinos-poet.com. No credit cards. Metro: Monastiraki. Map p 69.* ●

5 The Best of the **Outdoors**

Rambling on Filopappou

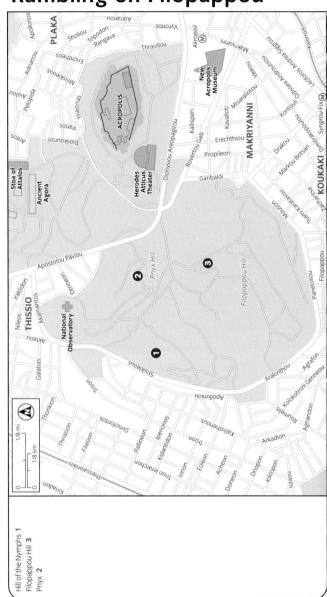

Hill of the Nymphs 1
Filopappou Hill 3
Pnyx 2

Three hills in central Athens—Filopappou, Pnyx, and the Hill of the Nymphs—have parks that face the Acropolis. Also known as the Hill of the Muses, Pnika, and Nymphon, respectively (and collectively known as Filopappou), these easy-to-get-to escapes in the middle of town are covered with pine forest. Most of all, superb views—of the city, the Parthenon, and the Saronic Gulf—can clearly be seen from each. START: **Metro to Thissio, or walk from the Acropolis, Areopagus, or Plaka.**

① Hill of the Nymphs. The cruciform (four-point) **National Observatory,** built in 1842, can clearly be seen on this hill, which slides into the districts of Thissio and Ano Petralona. Rising above the multidomed **Agia Marina** church, it was designed by Theophilos Hansen, architect of many other public buildings when the modern capital was in its infancy. The white ponies used to ferry tourists on horse-and-buggy rides can be seen grazing here off-hours, and you can wander the rock terrace that covers this hill. ⏱ *1–2 hr. Dionysiou Areopagitou/Apostolou Pavlou sts. Metro: Thissio.*

② Pnyx. The ancient **Assembly,** which moved here from the (now ancient) Agora, met in an amphitheater that faced the rock of the Areopagus. This is where Themistocles, Pericles, and Demosthenes commanded attention in the 4th and 5th centuries B.C. The semicircle was turned to face the other way in 404 B.C., when the audience's attention

waned, the Parthenon view too distracting even then. Have a seat on a park bench—or better yet, in the assembly—to rest. ⏱ *1–2 hr. Dionysiou Areopagitou/Apostolou Pavlou sts. Metro: Thissio.*

③ ★ Filopappou Hill. Great for picnics when the weather isn't too hot, the Hill of the Muses is topped by the night-lit Filopappou Monument, an A.D. 116 Pentelic marble tomb for the Roman consul of Athens, Julius Antiochus Philopappus, grandson of the last Greek Macedonian king of the Roman Syrian Commagene kingdom. (Got that?) It was from this vantage point that the Venetians bombed the intact Parthenon in 1687—and then quit the city 5 months later, carting off the Lion of Piraeus from then-named Porto Leone. Filopappou has a charming marble-and-tile path, as well as a central stone path, that meanders over the hill, past rock caves and monuments. ⏱ *1–2 hr. Dionysiou Areopagitou/Apostolou Pavlou sts. Metro: Thissio.*

The Agia Marina church was built on the site of an older church on the Hill of the Nymphs in 1922; the National Observatory is in the background.

Attica Zoological Park & First Cemetery

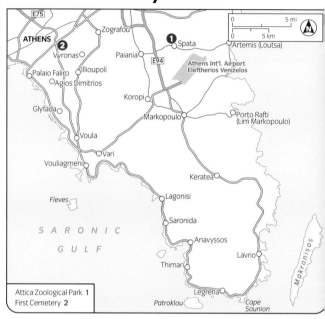

Attica Zoological Park 1
First Cemetery 2

While **thematically unrelated and geographically disparate,** the Athens municipal cemetery and the Athens zoo make excellent outdoorsy additions to any 3-day tour (see p 18). The First Cemetery, as it is called, contains impressive works of the plastic arts, where it seems like 19th-century sculptors competed to carve the most elaborate funerary statues possible, much like they did in antiquity. The Attica Zoological Park, on the other hand, is a little less morbid; it has an African savanna, a monkey jungle, and the third-largest bird collection in the world. START: **Metro to Syntagma.**

❶ ★★★ kids Attica Zoological Park. If you go to the zoo in each country you visit, as far as seeing caged animals is concerned, this one's not bad. It's also a calming diversion if you've got 2 or more hours to kill at the Venizelos Airport in Spata. The park is big, at 19 hectares (47 acres), has a large canteen, and is easy to get around, with stroller-friendly paths. Some 2,000 birds from more than 320 species vie for attention with the reptiles, and despite the fact that most of the 30-odd species of big game, such as zebra, lion, and giraffe, are usually sleeping (or bored-looking), there are many opportunities for animal-kingdom entertainment, especially in late spring. The monkeys will likely be the most fun, and alarming, as parents let their tots feed them by hand despite warning signs. Also alarming—and fascinating—is the collection of insects, including scorpions, moths, and butterflies. On-site is a children's playground for the very little, as mainly young families and couples go on Sundays (they can be found sitting on benches across from the big game). A gift shop sells postcards, T-shirts, and World Wildlife Fund toys, plus notebooks, key chains, and the like. 🕐 *3 hr. Yalou, Spata.* ☎ *210/ 663-4724. www.atticapark.com. Daily 9am–sunset. Admission 14€ adults, 10€ children 2–12 & seniors. Bus: 319 (from Doukissis Plakentias Metro Station, Christoupoli-bound) or take Attiki Odos national road from the airport to exit 18 (Spata) or from Elefsina to exit 16P (Rafina).*

② ★★★ **First Cemetery.** Not to be confused with the ancient cemetery of Kerameikos, Athens's 19th-century First Cemetery is a massive hilltop garden of olive and pine trees atop Ardittos Hill near Athens Stadium. It has acres of elaborate monuments and sculptures marking graves, including those of many Greek notables buried here. (National icon and actress Melina Mercouri, for instance, is buried near the entrance.) The most famous statue is by Tinos islander Yannoulis Halepas, whose *Sleeping Lady* (1877) is on

A giraffe, the tallest of all land-living animals, in repose at the Attica Zoological Park.

the tomb of Sophia Afentaki, the 18-year-old daughter of a wealthy Athenian. The cemetery does a healthy business, as Christian Orthodoxy does not allow cremation, only burial—so (very expensive) gravesites in the crowded graveyard are compact and usually rented for 3 years, when the bones are removed to an ossuary. If you own a mausoleum, however, your bones will stay put. Despite this busy cycle, the cemetery remains relaxing and beautiful. 🕐 *1 hr. Anapafseos & Trivonianou sts., Mets.* ☎ *210/923-6720. Apr–Oct 8am–8pm; Nov–Mar 8am– 5:30pm. Bus: A3, A4, 103, 108, 111, 155, 206, 208, 237, 856, 057, or 227 (to A' "Proto" Nekrotafio).*

Sleeping Lady, a monument in Athens's First Cemetery, depicts Sophia Afentaki, who died at only age 18.

The **Port of Piraeus**

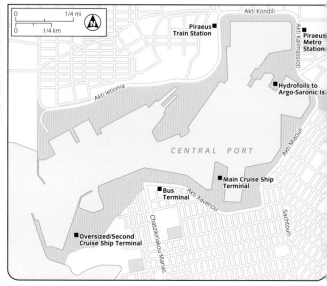

Angistri & Aegina

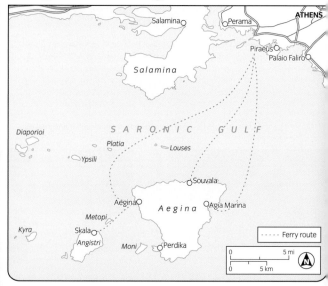

One of the world's busiest passenger ports, serving 19 million passengers annually, Athens's ancient harbor of Piraeus is a city in its own right, with picturesque wharves lined by fish-tavernas, bar-cafes, and yachts. It's where most tourists come to catch a ferry. Your first impression may be of a busy and dirty place, but if you enjoy seeing the "working" side of a town and being on the waterfront, with old warehouses and freighters visible at sea, then this is a good spot. And if spending more than an hour on a bus in heavy traffic en route to and/or from a coastal beach does not appeal, you have the pleasant option of taking a (frequent) boat to the beach at Angistri, a small pine-covered island in the Saronic Gulf. START: **Metro to Piraeus.**

① Piraeus. The port of Piraeus is an active and, yes, dirty place, its charming smaller harbors lined with everything from fishing boats to millionaires' yachts. It has a few restaurants along the docks, mostly mediocre and overpriced, and is difficult to navigate due to a lack of informative signs. But the main passenger port is a godsend for reaching the renowned Greek islands. (Extra points if you get to see an enormous ferry back into a tight slot and dock as easily as a car in a suburban driveway.) From central Athens, it takes 20 minutes to get there (take the Metro to Piraeus, cross the street, and you're in the port), so moving at a steady clip, you could be on a boat in 30. However, the absence of helpful signs at the main harbor and the constant hustle and bustle of Piraeus means you may want to give yourself extra time to catch your boat. ⏱ *30 min. Port Authority: 10 Akti Miaouli St.* ☎ *210/455-0229. www.olp.gr. Metro: Piraeus.*

② Angistri. If you want to combine a day at the beach with an island escape, boats leave from Piraeus port to Aegina or, even better, the little island of Angistri (Αγistri)—where there's nothing to do but read, sun, and swim. Angistri is 1 hour away by Flying Dolphin (hydrofoil), and 2-plus hours by regular ferry (the nicer way to go). The

beach is only a few feet from the dock, with umbrellas and sun beds for rent and tavernas and cafes across the "street." If you're unable to catch a direct boat from the mainland to Angistri, Flying Dolphins leave every hour from gate E8 in Piraeus to Aegina, where you can then catch a boat (every 15 min.) to Angistri. ⏱ *6 hr. Boat schedules: www.gtp.gr or www.openseas.gr. Tickets 14€ hydrofoil, 9€ ferry. Metro: Piraeus.*

A small sailboat moored off Aponissos in Angistri ("fishing hook"), on the Saronic Gulf.

The **South Coast Beaches**

Asteria Glyfada	**1**
Thalassea	**3**
Voula A'	**2**
Vouliagmeni	**4**
Yabanaki Varkiza	**5**

Summer holidays for Athenians typically involve sand and surf—which they bunk off to at the flimsiest excuse. In fact, some 60% of all Athenians take a summer holiday during the first 2 weeks of August. If you're here between June and August, when the temperature in the city may reach 46°C (115°F), you'll find that Athens, like Paris, belongs to the tourists. Those months might be a good time for you to get out of the city as well. Here are some popular fee-charging beaches along the Apollo Coast that have amenities, such as washrooms and umbrellas. And, yes, you can drink on the beach; no, don't go topless. START: **Metro to Syntagma.**

1 **kids** **Asteria Glyfada.** This beach across from the main seaside resort/suburb of Glyfada (17km/11 miles from Athens) was made popular when the old Athens airport was in the area in the 1980s. It went through a lull, but a revitalization effort a few years ago turned it back into a hot spot. It now has a Miami vibe, marked by white recliners, white umbrellas, white sand (artificially dumped on the beach and seabed), and clubs (including the Balux nightclub with live music). A string of canteens and bars serve drinks to you in your lounge chair. It's also the shopping, restaurant, and nightlife hub for suburbs farther along the coast. While the water here can be a bit shallow and murky, the facilities are nice and include hot showers, lockers for your valuables, a garden around

The resort town of Glyfada has several secluded beaches like this one, as well as the large modern Asteria Glyfada.

the beach, two minimarkets, and beach volleyball and soccer. ⏱ *2 hr. 58 Poseidonos Ave.* ☎ *210/894-4548. www.balux-septem.com. Daily 8:30am–9pm, beach bars 9am–1am. Admission 7€ weekdays, 11€ weekends/holidays, children half-price. Tram: Metaxa St. or bus: A1, A2, E1, E2, E22.*

② **kids** **Voula A'.** This beach, 19km/12 miles south of Athens in Voula, a suburban residential area neighboring the glitzy commercial area of Glyfada, is a big (300m/984 ft. by 30m/98 ft.), busy stretch of sand full of 20-somethings and teenagers. It's sandy, with pebbles in a few spots, but has little shade if you don't happen to snag a sun

bed. In addition to sun beds, you can find a swimming pool, a snack bar, water slides and watersports gear (skis, tubes, and boards), parachuting, pedal boats, racquetball, beach volleyball, minisoccer, some bars, and a minimarket. ⏱ *2 hr. 4 Alkyonidon St.* ☎ *210/895-9632. www.apollonies.gr. Daily 8am–sunset (beach closes); beachfront cafe & other facilities stay open at night. Admission 4€ adults, 1.50€ children 6–12 & seniors. Tram: Asklipiou Voulas St. or bus: A2, E1, E2, E22, 114, 116, 149, 340.*

③ **kids** **Thalassea.** Also known as Voula B', this is a smaller beach than Voula A' that was formerly run by the state. It lies a little farther down the coast (20km/12 miles from Athens), but it is quieter than Voula A', with calm, clear waters protected by concrete breakers. There's a snack bar, a minimarket, tennis courts, and a water slide. ⏱ *2 hr. 18 Alkyonidon St.* ☎ *210/895-9632. www.thalassea.gr. Daily 8am–sunset. Admission Mon–Fri 5€; Sat–Sun & holidays 6€; includes sun beds, umbrellas. Bus: A2, E1, E2, E22, 114, 116, 149, 340.*

④ **kids** **Vouliagmeni.** This is one of the most popular beach towns for Athenians (26km/16 miles away), as it's more like a resort. It's just past Voula, which is basically a suburb of

The marina of the Nautical Club of Vouliagmeni, one of the most exclusive in Greece.

The clear Saronic Gulf, off the town of Voula, was named for mythical King Saron, who drowned there while hunting a deer that had fled to the water.

Athens, but not quite as far as Varkiza, on an empty stretch of coastal road. It has a loyal following from before it was privatized, as it has lots of green areas and shade, and is well suited for young families and seniors. The beaches here are clean and clear, and Vouliagmeni has won a blue flag (a widely recognized eco-award) from the Foundation for the Environmental Education in Europe. The blue flag recognizes the quality of swimming water, absence of garbage, organization of the coast and safety of the visitors, and protection of nature and environmental education. There's also a marina in town, the country's most exclusive. Across the street, at Astir beach, are ruins of a temple to Apollo, if you didn't get enough archaeology from the Acropolis, but you have to pay to get in. The freshwater Lake Vouliagmeni, south of town, maintains a constant 24°C (75°F) temperature year-round and is known for its curative waters and a spa.

🕐 *2 hr. Poseidonos Ave.* ☎ *210/ 967- 3184. Entrance 4€, 60 & over, 6–12 years 1.50€. Bus: E22 or from Glyfada: 114, 116, 149.*

⑤ Yabanaki Varkiza. The farthest from Athens (30km/19 miles away) but the most pleasant in terms of seawater, sand, and gradient, Varkiza is along the road to Sounion. It's very popular, with rows of sun beds and blaring cafe-bars, and features cabanas, a self-service restaurant, a taverna, three beach bars, a water park, beach volleyball, windsurfing, water-skiing, and free parking. The drive to Varkiza affords a spectacular view of the cliffs of the Attica peninsula, while the return trip features a number of roadside tavernas offering roast lamb on a spit. Past Varkiza along the route to Cape Sounion are rocky coves, which can be great for snorkeling or swimming but are unsupervised.

🕐 *3 hr. Sounion Ave., Vari.* ☎ *210/ 897-2414. www.yabanaki.gr. Open May 1–Sept 30 daily 8am–8pm. Admission 5.50€ Mon–Fri; 7€ Sat– Sun; 3.50€ children 6–12, students & seniors; 5 & under free. Sat–Sun 4€ sun beds/umbrellas. Bus: E22, 170, 171, or 340.* ●

The rocky coves past Varkiza along the route to Cape Sounion offer opportunities for swimming and snorkeling but are unguarded.

Dining **Best Bets**

People dining in gentrified Psyrri, which is overflowing with bars, ouzeries, and cafes.

Best **Traditional Doughnuts**
Aigaion $ *46 Panepistimiou St. (p 15)*

Best **Exotic Food**
★ Altamira $$$ *36A Tsakalof St. (p 96)*

Best **Novel Greek Dining Experience**
★ Archaion Gefseis $$ *22 Kodratou St. (p 96)*

Best **High-Brow Evening Out**
★ Benaki Museum Thursday Night Buffet $$ *1 Koumbari St. (p 96)*

Best **French Bistro**
★ Chez Lucien $$ *32 Troon St. (p 96)*

Best Place for **Romance Without Breaking the Bank**
Filistron $$ *24 Apostolou Pavlou St. (p 97)*

Best Place for **Romance**
★★ GB Roof Garden $$$$ *Grande Bretagne Hotel, Syntagma Sq. (p 98)*

Best **Vegetarian Diner**
★ Health-Ecology $ *57 Panepistimiou St. (p 98)*

Best **Trendy Taverna**
Mamacas $$ *41 Persephonis St. (p 99)*

Best **Panorama of the City**
Orizontes $$$$$ *Aristippou & Ploutarchou sts. (p 99)*

Best Place to **Rub Shoulders with Locals**
★★ Papandreou's $ *Meat Market, Agora (p 100)*

Best **Meze**
★★ Rozalia $ *58 Valtetsiou St. (p 100)*

Best **Skewer Souvlaki**
Ta Souvlakis tou Hasapi $ *1 Apollonos St. (p 39)*

Best **Grill**
★★★ Telis $ *86 Evripidou St. (p 101)*

Best **Seafood**
★ Thalatta $$ *5 Vitonos St. (p 101)*

Best **Mince Souvlaki**
Thanasis $ *69 Mitropoleos St. (p 12)*

Best **People-Watching Taverna**
★ Vyzantino $$ *18 Kydathineon St. (p 102)*

Previous page: The Acropolis, as seen from the rooftop restaurant of the King George Palace hotel.

Lycabettus Dining

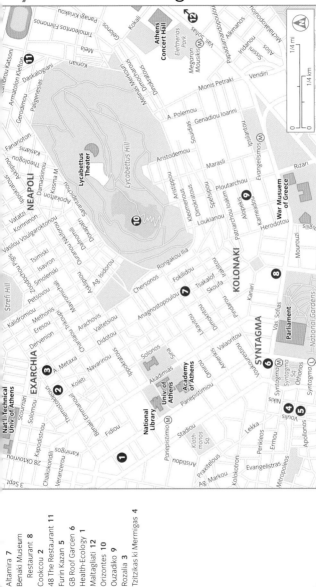

Psyrri & Plaka Dining

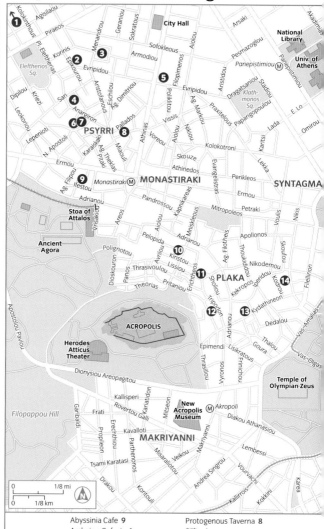

Abyssinia Cafe 9
Archaion Gefseis 1
Bar Guru Bar 3
Kouklis (Scholarhio) Ouzeri 12
Palea Athena 14
Papandreou's 5
Platanos Taverna 10

Protogenous Taverna 8
Silfio 6
Stamatopoulos 11
Telis 2
Vyzantino 13
Yoga Bala 4
Zeidoron 7

Gazi, Thissio & Koukaki Dining

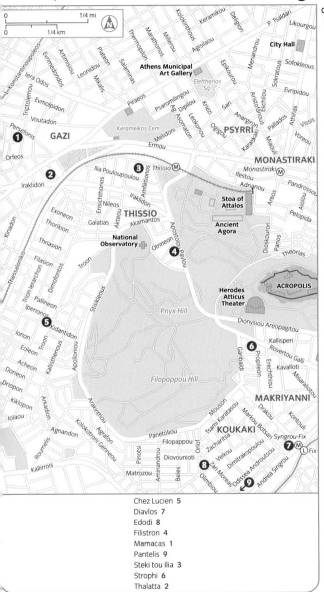

Chez Lucien **5**
Diavlos **7**
Edodi **8**
Filistron **4**
Mamacas **1**
Pantelis **9**
Steki tou Ilia **3**
Strophi **6**
Thalatta **2**

Athens Dining A to Z

★★ **Abyssinia Cafe** MONASTIRAKI *TAVERNA*   Unusual Greek dishes, a view of the Acropolis from upstairs, a lively atmosphere, and a somewhat off-the-restaurant-track "fleaville" location are the attractions at this mahogany-and-polished-copper cafe. *7 Kinetou St. at Abyssinia Sq. ☎ 210/ 321-7047. www.avissinia.gr. Entrees 10€. MC, V. Tues–Sat 11:30am–1am; Sun 11am–7pm; closed mid-July to Aug. Metro: Monastiraki. Map p 94.*

★ **Altamira** KOLONAKI *EXOTIC* Crocodile, reindeer, or ostrich, anyone? This bar-restaurant also serves dishes with Arabian, Indian, Mexican, and Southeast Asian pedigrees. *36A Tsakalof St. ☎ 210/361-4695 or 210/363-9906. Entrees 15€–20€. MC, V. Mon–Sat 1pm–1:30am; closed mid-July to Aug. Metro: Syntagma or bus: 200. Map p 93.*

★ **Archaion Gefseis** METAXOURGIO *TRADITIONAL GREEK*   "Ancient Flavors," including ambrosia of the gods, can be sampled at this theme restaurant that also re-creates dining in the distant past. The servers wear togas, but you don't have to. *22 Kodratou St. ☎ 210/523-9661. Entrees 15€. AE, DC, MC, V. Tues–Sat 7pm–1am; Sun noon–5pm; closed 2 weeks in Aug. Map 94.*

Bar Guru Bar AGORA *THAI* Whether you go for a craving or to try for the first time, any Thai specialty you could think of can be ordered at this bar-restaurant, despite being in a city where Southeast Asian ingredients aren't exactly ubiquitous. Martinis, highballs, and other cocktails await the adventurous. *10 Theatrou Sq. ☎ 210/324-6530. Entrees 15€. AE, DC, MC, V. Mon–Thurs 9:30pm–1am; Fri–Sat 9:30pm–1:30am. Metro: Omonia or Monastiraki. Map p 94.*

★ **Benaki Museum Restaurant** KOLONAKI *EUROPEAN*   Rest midtour with a quiche and an expansive view of Athens. The Thursday-night (8:30pm–midnight) buffet (40€ without drinks) is very popular, even with locals—reservations are recommended. *1 Koumbari St. at Vas. Sofias Ave. ☎ 210/367-1000. www. benaki.gr. Entrees 12€. AE, DC, MC, V. Open Mon, Wed & Fri–Sat 9am–5pm; Thurs 9am–midnight; Sun 9am–3pm; closed Tues, holidays. Metro: Syntagma. Map p 93.*

★ **Chez Lucien** ANO PETRALONA *FRENCH*   A blue, white, and red awning hides a tiny restaurant with a completely set table affixed to the ceiling. Since there's such limited

The chef at Archaion Gefseis has used archaeological records to prepare foods eaten in ancient Greece.

★ **Edodi** KOUKAKI *CONTEMPORARY* This is one of Athens's best restaurants, where the foodie chef brings ingredients to your table for precooking inspection, then gauges your tastes and prepares them accordingly. *Warning:* The restaurant is at the top of a steep staircase. *80 Veikou St.* ☎ *210/921-3013. Entrees 25€. AE, DC, MC, V. Mon–Sat 8pm–12:30am; closed July–Aug. Reserve ahead. Metro: Syngrou-Fix or trolley: 1, 5, 15. Map p 95.*

★ **Filistron** THISSIO *REGIONAL GREEK* This fits the bill in the romantic department: It's one of the best places in town to see the million-dollar view of the Acropolis and Lycabettus Hill while eating. *24 Apostolou Pavlou St.* ☎ *210/346-7554. Entrees 12€. DC, MC, V. Oct–May Tues–Sun noon–1am; Jun–Sept Tues–Sun 6pm–1am. Metro: Thissio. Map p 95.*

★ **48 The Restaurant** AMBE-LOKIPI *MODERN GREEK* For one of the best of Athens's "new cuisine" restaurants, try this place. The menu is daring and the decor is sleek. You can get finger food at the bar.

Filistron, as seen from Apostolou Pavlou Street, serves classic Greek dishes, as well as unusual regional Greek food.

space (you'll likely share a large table inside; there are more on the sidewalk), the French-country menu is limited as well—but always a tasty surprise. Reasonable prices, too, given the cuisine. *32 Troon St.* ☎ *210/346-4236. Entrees 14€. No credit cards. Daily 8:30pm–2am; closed Christmas week, 2 weeks at Easter, Aug. No reservations. Bus: 227. Map p 95.*

Cookcou EXARCHIA *EUROPEAN TRENDY* How else to describe this restaurant in the student district, where boho-looking waiters serve up things like Ho Chi Minh salad? *66 Themistokleous St.* ☎ *210/383-1955. Entrees 7€–11€. MC, V. Mon–Sat 1pm–1am. Metro: Omonia. Map 93.*

Diavlos KOUKAKI *GREEK/VEGETARIAN* Sample another facet of Greek life in this rustic establishment right at the Metro station, where Greek singers of old popular folk songs perform live during dinner. Try the vegetarian selections. *Warning:* It can get pretty raucous. *9 Drakou St.* ☎ *210/924-8737. Entrees 5€–6€; evening tickets 12€ except Wed–Thurs in winter (no shows). No credit cards. Daily 9am–2am. Metro: Syngrou-Fix. Map p 95.*

The radical interior of 48 The Restaurant was designed by Greek architectural firm ISV.

48 Armatolon & Klefton sts. ☎ *210/ 641-1082. www.48therestaurant.com. Entrees 30€–35€. AE, DC, MC, V. Mon–Sat 8:30pm–12:30am; closed July–Aug, Sun & holidays. Metro: Ambelokipi. Map p 93.*

Furin Kazan SYNTAGMA *JAPA- NESE* Get your Japanese-food fix at this well-placed restaurant that straddles the town center and Plaka. It's got an extensive menu and reasonable prices, even if the portions are smaller than you may be used to. *2 Apollonos St.* ☎ *210/ 322-9170. Entrees 20€. AE, DC, MC, V. Mon–Sat noon–11:30pm; Sun 2–11:30pm. Metro: Syntagma. Map p 93.*

★★ GB Roof Garden SYNTAGMA *MEDITERRANEAN* This is a destina- tion restaurant with a to-die-for view favored by politicians from nearby Parliament and those about to leave singledom behind. It's open year- round for breakfast, lunch, and din- ner on the eighth floor of the city's most prestigious hotel. The Italian chef makes pastas, plus fish and steak, and there are homemade desserts. Or just come for the sun- set and have a drink at the translu- cent backlit bar, which is open-air in summer. *Grande Bretagne Hotel, Syntagma Sq.* ☎ *210/333-0000.*

The traditional Greek salad is made with chopped tomatoes, cucumber, red onion, bell peppers, Kalamata olives, feta cheese, and dressed with olive oil.

Scholarhio, as it's commonly known, serves meze dishes, such as fried egg- plant or marinated peppers.

www.grandebretagne.gr. Entrees 25€–40€. AE, DC, MC, V. Daily 6:30–11am & 1pm–1:15am; New Year's Eve 8pm–3:30am; New Year's Day 1–4pm; reduced holiday hours. Metro: Syntagma. Map p 93.

★ Health-Ecology OMONIA *VEGETARIAN* This cafeteria has been serving cheap, Greek-style dishes and fresh juices for years. There's a health-food store attached. *57 Panepistimiou St.* ☎ *210/321- 0966. Entrees 4€–6€. No credit cards. Mon–Fri 8am–9:30pm; Sat 8am–8pm; Sun 10am–4pm; closed holidays. Metro: Omonia. Map p 93.*

Kouklis (Scholarhio) Ouzeri PLAKA *MEZE/TAVERNA* Choose from a tray of appetizers at this tourist-oriented taverna, nicknamed the Scholarhio for the nearby school. Ten dishes, a liter of wine (or a substi- tute), mineral water, and dessert go for 12€ per person for a group of four or more. *14 Tripodon St.* ☎ *210/ 324-7605. www.sholarhio.gr. Meze 2.50€–5€. MC, V. Daily 11am–2am. Metro: Syntagma or Monastiraki. Map p 94.*

Restaurant Fast Facts

Eating out is a national pastime in Athens, and piled-up, fresh ingredients are the staples of Greek cooking. Athenian dining, like its shopping, is sometimes divided by neighborhood (a good midday or early-evening souvlaki can always be found on "Kebab Street" at the foot of Mitropoleos St. at Monastiraki Sq.; the Psyrri district often has live *bouzouki* music to go with a later 10pm dinner). Most restaurants, except those in hotels and those that cater to tourists, are usually closed on either Sunday, Monday, or Tuesday, as well as on Christmas, New Year's Day, Easter, and around August 15 (the Assumption of the Virgin Mary). Unless stated otherwise, the closing times listed are when the kitchen closes, not the restaurant—it is a rare proprietor who would kick out a patron. As for tipping, restaurants may include a service charge, but an extra 10% to 15% for the waiter or busboy is appreciated.

★★ **Maltagliati** PANORMOU *ITALIAN* A small trattoria in Panormou draws a crowd with its homemade pastas and other delicacies from across the Adriatic. *6 Varnakioti St.* ☎ *210/691-6676. Entrees 10€. No credit cards. Mon–Sat 8pm–midnight; closed Aug. Metro: Panormou. Map p 93.*

Mamacas GAZI *MODERN GREEK* This upscale taverna gets great reviews, more for its location. You can get a good meal with out-of-the-ordinary dishes while sidewalk dining beside Kerameikos Metro station in trendy Gazi. *41 Persephonis St.* ☎ *210/346-4984. www.mamacas.gr. Entrees 11€–16€. Daily 1:30pm–1:30am. AE, MC, V. Metro: Kerameikos. Map p 95.*

Orizontes KOLONAKI *CONTINENTAL* See the city in all its enormity and gaze out to sea, freighters and all, from this seafood restaurant atop Lycabettus Hill, owned by a chain that has its own fish farms. **Cafe Lycabettus,** a Mediterranean bar-restaurant with a cheaper menu, is at the same site. *Aristippou & Ploutarchou sts.* ☎ *210/721-0701.*

A meal at Orizontes might include crayfish risotto or braised lamb shank.

www.kastelorizo.com.gr. *Entrees 30€–40€; cafe entrees 15€.* AE, MC, V. *Daily 9am–2am. Bus: 022, 060, 200 to the cable railway. Map p 93.*

Ouzadiko KOLONAKI *MEZE* The shopping mall location may be odd, but this lively *ouzeri* (meze-type restaurant) has a wide variety of food, and of course, ouzo. *Lemos International Centre, 25–29 Karneadou St.* ☎ *210/729-5484. Entrees 16€.* AE, DC, MC, V. *Mon–Sat 12:30pm–midnight; closed Christmas, New Year's Day, Easter & Aug. Metro: Evangelismos. Map p 93.*

Palea Athena PLAKA *TAVERNA* The prices are just fine and the selection is wider than usual—including something that fails entry on most menus: soup—at this old-fashioned Athenian restaurant. *46 Nikis St.* ☎ *210/324-5777. Entrees 6€.* AE, DC, MC, V. *Daily noon–12:30am. Metro: Syntagma. Map p 94.*

★★ Pantelis PALAIO FALIRO *TRADITIONAL GREEK* Those who have seen the Greek film *A Touch of Spice* can easily (on the pocket) indulge at this restaurant that makes, well, spicier food. *96 Naiadon St.* ☎ *210/982-5512. Entrees 11€. No credit cards. Daily 8pm–midnight; closed holidays, part of Aug. Tram: Panagitsa. Map p 95.*

★★ Papandreou's AGORA *TAVERNA* This *mageiria* ("cookhouse") serves big portions of soups, stews, and square meals round-the-clock near one of the meat-market entrances at the Central Market. Customers range from surly loners to loud clubgoers who happily rub shoulders in the name of taste. *1 Aristogeitonos St. at Evripidou St. (inside the Agora meat market).* ☎ *213/008-2242. Entrees 6€.* V. *Daily 24 hr. Metro: Omonia, Panepistimiou, or Monastiraki. Map 94.*

Platanos Taverna PLAKA *TAVERNA* Platanos is a simple classic Greek taverna on a quiet street near the Tower of the Winds. You can eat inside or outside. *4 Dioyenous St.* ☎ *210/322-0666. Entrees 8€–9€. No credit cards. Mon–Sat noon–4:30pm & 7:30pm–midnight; closed Sun, 2 weeks in Aug. Metro: Monastiraki or Syntagma. Map p 94.*

Protogenous Taverna PSYRRI *MEZE/TAVERNA* "Primary" is a good choice to try a variety of dishes that you wouldn't normally find in a taverna. *10 Protogenous St.* ☎ *210/322-8658. Entrees 11€. No credit cards. Winter: Mon–Fri noon–5pm, Fri–Sat 8:30pm–2am w/live bouzouki; summer: Mon–Fri noon–5pm; closed Sun, Jan 1, Easter, 2 weeks in Aug & Dec 25. Metro: Monastiraki. Map p 94.*

★★ Rozalia EXARCHIA *MEZE/TAVERNA* Take your choice of meze off a tray and/or order entrees in the enclosed garden (opposite the taverna) at this busy restaurant off Exarchia Sq. *58 Valtetsiou St.* ☎ *210/330-2933. Entrees 6€–8€.* DC, MC, V.

The spanakorizo (spinach risotto) at Rozalia makes a good meze starter.

Greek moussaka consists of layers of ground lamb or beef, sliced eggplant, and tomato, topped with a white sauce and baked.

Daily 11am–2am; closed Jan 1, Dec 25. Metro: Omonia. Map p 93.

Silfio PSYRRI *MODERN GREEK* The cat-and-moon-silhouette logo is a beacon in the Psyrri maze: It's notably reliable for big portions, tasty food, and good service. *24 Taki St.* ☎ *210/324-7028. Entrees 14€. AE, DC, MC, V. Mon 5:30pm till late; Tues–Sun noon–2am; closed Easter. Metro: Thissio. Map p 94.*

★ **Steki tou Ilia** THISSIO *TAVERNA* A duo of traditional tavernas under one name on the same pedestrian street, this place has excellent lamb chops, and the waiters scurry across the road back and forth to serve them. *5 Eptahalkou St.* ☎ *210/345-8052; 7 Thessalonikis St.* ☎ *210/342-2407. Entrees 7€–10€. No credit cards. Mon–Sat 1pm–1am; Sun 1–5:30pm; closed Jan 1, Easter & Dec 25. Eptahalkou closed last 2 weeks in Aug; Thessalonikis closed first 2 weeks in Aug. Metro: Thissio. Map p 95.*

Strophi MAKRIYANNI *TAVERNA* Like visiting your disheveled grandpa or donning a well-worn shoe, this is a sure-bet classic Greek taverna in an area short of restaurants. *25 Rovertou*

Galli St. ☎ *210/921-4130. Entrees 12€. MC, V. Mon–Sat 7pm–1am; closed Sun, Jan 1, Easter & Dec 25. Bus: 230. Map p 95.*

★★★ **Telis** PSYRRI *GRILL* Within moments of your sitting down at Telis, a stack of chops appears on the table—possibly the best pork chops in Athens. The ultimate for hungry carnivores. *86 Evripidou St. at Koumoundourou Sq.* ☎ *210/324-2775. Entrees 7€. No credit cards. Mon–Sat 11am–2am; closed Sun, part of Aug. Bus: 100, 200. Map p 94.*

★ **Thalatta** THISSIO/GAZI *SEAFOOD* Sate your raw-oyster craving in this restaurant opened by a former sea-farer obsessed with freshness. Other seafood, including fish, clams, sea urchin, and octopus, are fresh daily, straight from the Aegean. *5 Vitonos & 105 Piraeos sts., Gefyra Poulopoulou.* ☎ *210/346-4204. Entrees 10€. AE, DC, MC, V. Nov–Apr Mon–Sat 8pm–1:30am; Sun noon–6pm; closed Jan 1, Good Friday, Easter, Dec 25 & Aug. Metro: Kerameikos or Thissio or bus/trolley: B18, G18, 21, 035, 049, 227, 400. Map p 95.*

Provisions decorate the walls of Tzitzikas ki Mermigas, which is reminiscent of a country kitchen or general store.

★ Tzitzikas ki Mermigas
SYNTAGMA *MODERN GREEK* Eat in an "olde grocery store" and sample any kind of Greek cuisine (cooked, baked, or grilled) indoors or on the sidewalk. The tables have butcher paper on top and drawers with flatware and napkins. *12–14 Mitropoleos St.* ☎ *210/324-7607. Entrees 11€. MC, V. Mon–Sat 1pm–1am; closed holidays, 2 weeks in Aug. Metro: Syntagma. Map p 93.*

★ Vyzantino
PLAKA *TAVERNA* The best place in Plaka for people-watching and meeting friends over a hearty daily lunch special is at this easily found and well-known place, popular with both locals and tourists for its traditional fare. *18 Kydathineon St.* ☎ *210/322-7368. Entrees 10€. AE, DC, MC, V. Daily 7am–1am. Metro: Syntagma. Map p 94.*

Yoga Bala PSYRRI *INDIAN* The main favorites from the subcontinent have been adapted for milder palates, deeper pockets, and vegetarians here. *5–7 Riga Palamidou St.* ☎ *210/331-1335. Entrees 8€–16€. MC, V. Tues–Sat 8pm–1am; closed Sun–Mon, July–Aug. Bar open all year. Metro: Monastiraki or Thissio. Map p 94.*

Zeidoron PSYRRI *MEZE* Choose from a wide variety of wine, beer, and ouzo, plus excellent meze and heartier fare, at this restaurant better known for its central Psyrri locale. *10 Taki St. at Agia Anargyron St.* ☎ *210/321-5368. Entrees 11€. AE, MC, V. Mon–Thurs 6pm–2am; Fri–Sun noon–2am; closed Jan 1, Good Friday, Easter Monday, 1 week in Aug & Dec 25. Metro: Monastiraki. Map p 94.* ●

Outdoor diners at Vyzantino, which serves roast pork, lamb, moussaka, and other taverna staples.

Nightlife Best Bets

The racy and fun atmosphere inside Destijl, a club with a winter location in Psyrri.

Best Glamorous Seaside Lounge
★ Akrotiri Lounge, *B5 Vas. Georgiou St. (p 108)*

Best Hotel Bar
★ Alexander's Bar, *Hotel Grande Bretagne, Syntagma Sq. (p 109)*

Best Place to Go Clubbing
★★ Destijl, *Iroon Sq. (p 112)*

Best Bar with a Panoramic View
★ Galaxy Bar, *Hilton Hotel, 46 Vas. Sofias Ave. (p 109)*

Best Cafe-Bar for People-Watching
Jackson Hall, *4 Milioni St. (p 108)*

Best Urban Watering Hole
★★ Kafeneion Pente Dromous, *Themistokleous and Koletti sts. (p 109)*

Best Metro Station Bar
Mamacas, *41 Persefonis St. (p 110)*

Best (and Only) Irish Bar
Mike's Irish Bar, *6 Sinopis St. (p 110)*

Best Place to Mix with Athenian Youth
Podilato, *48 Themistokleous St. (p 111)*

Best Place to See a Big-Name Greek Singer
Rex, *48 Panepistimiou St. (p 114)*

Best Authentic Bouzouki
★ Romeo, *1 Ellinikou St. (p 114)*

Best Cafe-Bar for Alt Rock
★ Stavlos, *10 Iraklidon St. (p 108)*

Best Layout
★★★ Thirio, *1 Lepeniotou St. (p 112)*

Previous page: Striking horse lamps designed by Front for Moooi greet visitors to T-Palace.

Lycabettus Nightlife

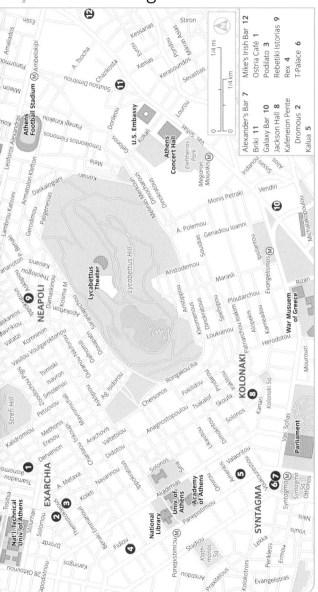

Alexander's Bar 7	Mike's Irish Bar 12
Briki 11	Ostria Café 1
Galaxy Bar 10	Podilato 3
Jackson Hall 8	Rebetiki Istorias 9
Kafeneion Pente	Rex 4
Dromous 2	T-Palace 6
Kalua 5	

Psyrri & Plaka Nightlife

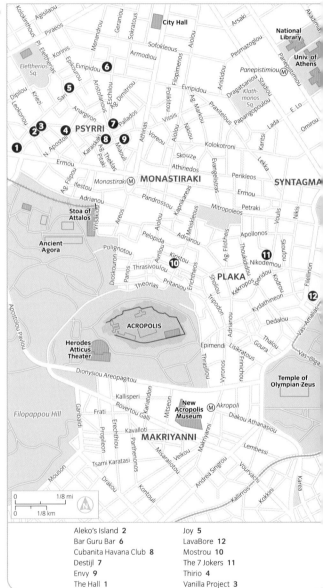

Gazi & Thissio Nightlife

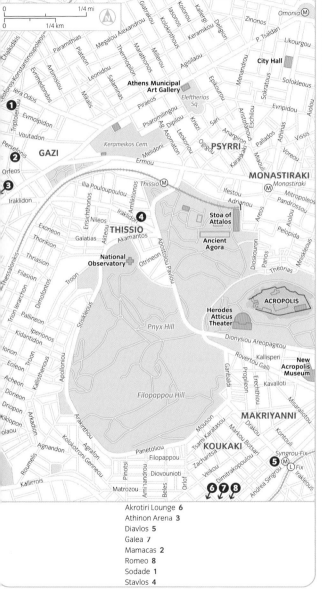

Akrotiri Lounge **6**
Athinon Arena **3**
Diavlos **5**
Galea **7**
Mamacas **2**
Romeo **8**
Sodade **1**
Stavlos **4**

Athens Nightlife A to Z

Bar- & Club-Restaurants

★ **Akrotiri Lounge** AGIOS KOS-MAS   The food at this glam seaside lounge-bar-restaurant is various and artful, ranging from lamb to caviar, as is the music, which plays the gamut from Greek to hip-hop and R&B. It's about 6.8km (4¼ miles) from central Athens, along the coast. *B5 Vas. Georgiou St., Kalamaki.* ☎ *210/985-9147. www. akrotirilounge.gr. Nov–Apr Fri–Sat 15€ cover; May–Oct Mon–Thurs 15€ cover, Fri–Sun 20€ cover. Tram: 2nd Agia Kosma or bus: A1, A2. Map p 107.*

Cubanita Havana Club PSYRRI   Cuban cuisine, cigars, and the perfect mojito are coupled with live Latin music by Oscar Ponse's house band and the accompanying dancers. This place is small, but it's the spot for salsa. *28 Karaiskaki St. at Psyrri Sq.* ☎ *210/331-4605. www. cubanita.gr. Closed Aug. 15€ cover w/drink. Metro: Monastiraki. Map p 106.*

The Cubanita Havana Club is small but lively, and the best place for Latin dancing in the city.

Stavlos is part restaurant, bar, lounge, and even art gallery—it hosts exhibitions and film screenings.

Jackson Hall KOLONAKI   The best-known bar-cafe-restaurant in dress-up Kolonaki isn't Athenian at all—it's dedicated to American memorabilia and simple American-style food such as burgers and steaks. The crowd, however, is fashionably European, including the models that serve the food and populate the bar. Sit out on the pedestrian sidewalk near the main square to people-watch. *4 Milioni St.* ☎ *210/361-6098. Metro: Syntagma. Map p 105.*

★ **Stavlos** THISSIO   This easygoing rock bar, restaurant, and cafe complex converted from the former royal stables is an anchor establishment on cafe-lined Iraklidon Street. The cafe is calmer than the bar, if you want to sit for a drink, but the hipster beats make this a fine place to rock out (though only ever as good as the DJ). Some nights feature an open mic or gallery exhibits. *10 Iraklidon St.* ☎ *210/346-7206 or 210/345-2502. Metro: Thissio. Map p 107.*

Bars & Lounges

★ **Alexander's Bar** SYNTAGMA An 18th-century tapestry depicting Alexander the Great dominates this classic, piano-entertained hotel bar where you can order Dom Pérignon by the glass. It was cited as one of the best hotel bars in the world by Forbes.com, and the upscale clientele—drawn by the cigar list and vast liquor selection—reflects this. *Hotel Grande Bretagne, Syntagma Sq.* ☎ *210/333-0000. www.grande bretagne.gr. Open from 10am. Metro: Syntagma. Map p 105.*

★ **Bar Guru Bar** AGORA The small and friendly bar upstairs from the Thai restaurant of the same name plays anything from jazz to dub (remixed reggae). The Chinese lanterns and paper flowers give an authentic Asian flair. *10 Theatrou Sq.* ☎ *210/324-6530. Metro: Omonia or Monastiraki. Map p 106.*

Briki MAVILI SQUARE The popular art/freestyle bar in the Embassy district no longer just attracts bohemians. It's tiny, but a good place to start your night. *6 Dorilaiou St.* ☎ *210/645-2380. Closed Jan 1, Easter, 2 weeks in Aug. Metro: Megaron Mousikis. Map p 105.*

★ **Galaxy Bar** HILTON A gorgeous view of the Acropolis, smart decor, perfect cocktails, and a spot on the top floor of the city's most iconic hotel mark this celebrity-frequented wood-bedecked bar. *Hilton Athens, 46 Vas. Sofias Ave.* ☎ *210/728-1000. Metro: Evangelismos. Map p 105.*

★ **Joy** PSYRRI This is a fun little modern-art bar on the third floor of a neoclassical building, above the Beer Academy restaurant. Its various small rooms have sparse industrial decor in shades of gray. There's live music on Thursdays. *18 Sarri & 2 Sachtouri sts.* ☎ *210/322-8038. Opens at midnight daily. Occasional cover 10€ w/1st drink. Metro: Monastiraki or Thissio. Map p 106.*

★★ **Kafeneion Pente Dromous** EXARCHIA Get a taste of the typical urban environment at this buzzing

The rooftop terrace of Galaxy Bar, in the landmark Hilton Athens, is popular with celebrities and guests of the hotel.

Athens by Night

Cafes, bars, and clubs are almost as common as eating establishments in Athens, and since it's one of the safest cities in the world for walking at night (traffic excepted), it would be a shame to miss out on the nightlife. The places listed in this chapter are open year-round unless stated otherwise. (Some may close during the month of Aug, when the rest of Athens flees for the shoreline.) To keep abreast of what's going on when, look for weekly listings magazines around town, such as **Athinorama** (www.athinorama.gr). These are in Greek, but foreign acts or DJs are usually noted in Latin letters, or enlist help from a Greek-speaker. Also try websites such as **www.athens nights.gr** or **www.e-djs.gr** to see who's playing where. A few final words of advice: If you see people drinking bottled beverages, follow suit and don't drink the hard stuff on tap, which may be a cheap (and serious hangover-causing) substitute. Also, in most places you can reserve a table with a bottle of whiskey to share (for four people and up) for around 110€. Finally, many venues change locations and/or names from one year to the next as well as seasonally.

mainstream bar with a cafe feel (it also serves meze) on the ground floor of an apartment building.

Even the sign has an island feel at Mamacas, which attracts a hip crowd with its good but expensive food and packed bar.

Themistokleous & Koletti sts. ☎ *210/380-0642. Daily 10am till late. Metro: Omonia. Map p 105.*

Mamacas GAZI   This island-atmosphere all-white bar attracts the stylish who like to mingle. There's a same-name taverna restaurant across the street that attracts the hungry—in fact, the taverna came first, inspired by the owners' mothers' cooking (*mamacas* means "mommies"). *41 Persefonis St.* ☎ *210/346-4984. www.mamacas.gr. Bar open daily 10pm till late (4–5am on weekends). Metro: Kerameikos. Map p 107.*

Mike's Irish Bar AMBELOKIPI Athens's Irish bar has the staples—darts and a few Irish singing acts—as well as some non-Irish additions (seven TVs; a big screen; karaoke; and live rock, disco, and funk). *6 Sinopis St. behind Athens Tower.* ☎ *210/777-6797. Open Mon–Fri from 8pm; Sat–Sun from 3pm; closed Aug. Cover 3€ for karaoke night &*

Podilato means "bicycle" in Greek, and that's the main feature of this small, easygoing student bar.

6€ for live shows. Metro: Ambelokipi or trolley: 3, 7, 8, 13 or bus: 230, 408, 419, 450, 550. Map p 105.

Ostria Cafe EXARCHIA   Just off Exarchia Square, the front courtyard of this overlooked cafe is a pleasant place to settle into with a drink in summer; the inside feels more like a

restaurant. 65 Themistokleous St. ☎ 210/330-0907. Metro: Omonia or bus: 035, 060, 200, 224, A7, B7, E7. Map p 105.

Podilato EXARCHIA   You can't help but mingle with the student-locals at this cute little ground-level bar with old-fashioned floor tiles,

Casino Action

Greeks love to gamble, and there are two casinos near Athens. One is the **Club Hotel Casino Loutraki,** on 48 Poseidonos Ave. (☎ 27440/65-501; www.clubhotelloutraki.gr or www.casinoloutraki.gr), in the seaside resort town of the same name, 80km (50 miles) from Athens. The whole complex has 80 games, 1,000 slot machines, a swish hotel, a restaurant, and a spa. The resort also attracts many older visitors due to its curative hot springs. The hotel's own Casino Express bus to and from Athens is 15€ (☎ 210/523-4188 or 210/523-4144), and includes casino entrance, drinks on the gaming floors, and a meal at the Neptune restaurant. The other casino, the **Regency Casino Mont Parnes,** on Mount Parnitha (www.regency.gr), is recovering from the devastating fires of 2007 and has been publicity shy (there's no contact info) during its rebuilding since the Regency group was awarded the former state-owned facility. After renovation, it will have 53 table games and 508 slot machines. A cable car takes you up to the hotel from the base of the mountain in Aharnon in northern Athens (18km/11 miles from central Athens), or you can drive there (30km/19 miles).

The avant-garde layout of the T-Palace bar in the King George Palace Hotel was designed by Greek film director Antonis Kalogridis.

vinyl seats, and a crowd. *48 Themistokleous St.* ☎ *210/330-3430. Metro: Omonia. Map p 105.*

The 7 Jokers SYNTAGMA This intimate (read: small) after-hours bohemian bar hosts clubbers chilling out to reggae and funk. You can also get a glass of good whiskey. *7 Voulis St.* ☎ *210/321-9225. Open daily. Metro: Syntagma. Map p 106.*

★★★ **Thirio** PSYRRI This unusual but casual bar covers two levels. The myriad seating is divided into little cubbyhole spaces, room after room, lit by candles and decorated with African tribal artifacts. The sum effect is curious but unthreatening and inviting. There's even some space in which to dance to the ethnic music. *1 Lepeniotou St.* ☎ *210/ 321-7836. Mon 8:30pm till late; Tues–Sun 3:30pm till late. Metro: Monastiraki. Map p 106.*

T-Palace SYNTAGMA The oddly named and uniquely decorated black-and-white lounge bar is a very classy central place to meet (it's on Syntagma Sq.). It's as popular as it is accessible, and serves light meals, though eating in the postmodern room seems disconcerting. *King George Palace Hotel, 3 Vas. Georgiou St. at Syntagma Sq.* ☎ *210/325-0504. www.classicalhotels.com. Metro: Syntagma. Map p 105.*

Dance Clubs

★★ **Destijl** PSYRRI A clubber's club that moved from the south coast to the party island of Mykonos, it now has a winter home in nightlife central: Psyrri. There's great music and a good party atmosphere but the club also has strict face control at the door and recommends reservations. *Iroon Sq.* ☎ *210/960-2611, 210/895-9645, or 6944/654-019. Daily 9pm till late. Wed–Thurs & Sun 10€ cover w/drink; Fri–Sat 15€. Metro: Monastiraki. Map p 106.*

★ **Envy** PSYRRI This big mainstream club caters to rich, trendy youth, with heavies at the door, hip-hop and R&B on Wednesday, and Greek music on Sunday. Like a true Athenian, the whole thing moves to the island of Paros in summer. *Monastiraki Center, 3 Agias Eleousis St.* ☎ *210/331-7801 or 210/331-7802. www.dubliner.gr. Daily from*

Envy draws a crowd of wealthy youth, so it's a good idea to make an advance reservation.

Nightlife Districts

Depending on the neighborhood, Athens bars can have a real cosmopolitan international feel or a traditional Greek tilt. For example, there are many English or foreign bars around Grigoriou Lambraki Street in **Glyfada,** in the southern suburbs of Athens. The big dance clubs operate in summer on the **Poseidonos (Apollo) coast.** In town, around **Exarchia Square,** you'll find a heavy student crowd, while on **Milioni Street** and at the end of **Haritos Street** you'll see a sophisticated dressed-up clientele. **Plaka** is filled with casual cafe-bars at the squares, and **Thissio** has similar outdoor cafe-bars along pedestrian Iraklidon and Apostolou Pavlou streets. The up-and-coming gay area of Athens is now **Gazi,** which has restaurants, bars, and clubs where there once were factories. The **Ilissia** area (near the Hilton), **Alexandras Avenue** (between the Metro station and Kifissias Ave.), and **Kifissia,** in the northern suburbs, all also sport vibrant bar scenes. **Psyrri,** however, is *the* nightlife district for any age. It was formerly populated by tradesmen during the day and a decidedly rougher crowd at night, but is now the mainstream place to go, with restaurants, bars, clubs, and cafes.

midnight. *Wed–Thurs & Sun 10€ cover; Fri–Sat 15€. Reservations recommended. Metro: Monastiraki. Map p 106.*

★★ **Galea** GLYFADA   This is one of the hottest spots in Athens. A very attractive (and beautiful-people attracting) seaside dance club, it plays mainstream music with the usual hip-hop, R&B, and Greek nights. It moves to a different seaside location each summer. *Oct–Apr: Oscar's Shopping Mall, 9 Sisimopoulou St., 2nd floor.* ☎ *210/894-4990. www. galea.gr. Call for hours. 10€ cover w/drink. Bus: A2. Map p 107.*

The Hall THISSIO   The former Luv club is a popular (and convenient) dance hall (read: huge warehouse) that hosts foreign guest DJs and well-known local ones. *1 Asomaton Sq. at Ermou St.* ☎ *210/322-4553. Open Fri–Sat year-round. Cover from 20€, depending on event. Metro: Thissio. Map p 106.*

Kalua SYNTAGMA   One of the city's oldest, this busy basement club-disco is located on its own in downtown Athens, but that hasn't dampened its popularity. *6 Amerikis St.* ☎ *210/360-8304. Daily from midnight. 15€ cover. Metro: Syntagma. Map p 105.*

★ **LavaBore** ZAPPEION   An enduring if cheesy dance spot with little face control, this is suitable for budget travelers. It plays popular foreign music and switches to Greek near closing, like most other foreign-music bars and clubs. *25 Filellinon St.* ☎ *210/324-5335. Daily Feb–Nov; closed Dec–Jan. 10€ cover w/drink. Metro: Syntagma. Map p 106.*

Vanilla Project PSYRRI   Another spot for glam Athenians, this friendly bar, club, and restaurant has two stages (drink and see a show) and a dance area. *37 Sarri St.* ☎ *210/322-0647. Closed July–Aug.*

15€ cover w/drink. Metro: Monastiraki. Map p 106.

Gay & Lesbian

Aleko's Island PSYRRI   This well-known, mainstream gay bar has moved from its longtime Kolonaki-area location to Psyrri. Not too dark, not too loud, but it still looks like a meat market. It plays mostly lounge music. *41 Sarri St. No phone. Daily from 9pm. Metro: Syntagma. Map p 106.*

Sodade GAZI   This bar-club-lounge plays cool house in two rooms in the gay-friendly district of Gazi. *10 Triptolemou St. ☎ 210/ 346-8657. www.sodade.gr. Closed Good Friday. 8€ cover. Metro: Kerameikos. Map p 107.*

Live Greek Music

Athinon Arena GAZI   If you have deep pockets and want to see a big-name Greek singer, try this place, which at the time of writing was featuring Marinella and Antonis Remos, kind of Vegas-style. A bottle of wine

Late-night dancing and partying at Romeo, which serves up live music after-hours.

for two is 100€, a bottle of whiskey 180€. *166 Piraeos St. ☎ 210/347-1111. Open Nov–Apr Thurs–Sat. 20€ cover, depending on day/season. Bus: 049, 815, 914. Map p 107.*

Mostrou PLAKA   This *laika*, a popular urban "stage" club, is big for Plaka but small for its purpose: hosting well-known Greek performers. For a bit of fresh air, there's a roof garden bar and restaurant. *22 Mnissikleos St. at Lysiou St. ☎ 210/ 322-5558 or 210/322-5337. Open daily mid-Apr to end of Oct 6pm– 2am or later (live music begins at 8:15pm); Greek performances Nov– Apr Fri–Sun. A la carte dinner 30€; wine & meze (to share) 75€; drinks 10€. Metro: Monastiraki. Map p 106.*

Rebetiki Istoria NEAPOLI This established venue serves up dinner as well as really good *rebetika* (early-20th-century urban lower-class *bouzouki* music). *181 Ippokratous St. ☎ 210/642-4937. Daily Sept–Easter Tues–Sun; June Fri–Sat; closed July–Aug. 6€ cover w/drink. Bus: 230. Map p 105.*

Rex OMONIA   The current show home of Greek singers Eleftheria Arvanitaki and Dimitra Galinia is conveniently located downtown. *48 Panepistimiou St. ☎ 210/381-4591. Daily Nov–Apr Thurs–Sun. 20€ cover w/drink. Metro: Omonia. Map p 105.*

★ **Romeo** ELLINIKO   This very accessible (that is, of lower cost) and fun Greek-music dance hall on the coast lets you get up and dance on the tables. If that's not your style, you can also buy baskets of flowers to shower on the singers and impromptu dancers. *1 Ellinikou St. ☎ 210/894-5345 or 210/894-1893. Daily Thurs–Sat. 15€ cover w/drink. Tram: Ellinon Olympionikon or bus: A1, A2. Map p 107.*

Arts & Entertainment **Best Bets**

Best **Free Art Gallery**
Athens Municipal Art Gallery, *51 Piraeos St. (p 120)*

Best **Use of an Olympic Venue**
★ Badminton Theater, *Kannelopoulou (Katehaki) Ave. (p 126)*

Best Place to **See Greek Folk Dance**
★★ Dora Stratou Theatre, *Filopappou Hill (p 122)*

Best Place to **See an Ancient Play**
★★★ Epidaurus Theater, *Epidavros (p 122)*

Best **Jazz Club**
Half Note Jazz Club, *17 Trivonianou St. (p 124)*

Best **High-Brow Evening Out**
★★★ Herodes Atticus Theater, *Acropolis (p 122)*

Best **Concert Hall**
★ Megaron Mousikis, *Vas. Sofias and Kokkali sts. (p 123)*

Best **Low-Brow Evening Out**
★★ Stamatopoulos Taverna, *26 Lissiou St. (p 123)*

Best **Exhibition Space**
★★ Technopolis, *100 Piraeos St. (p 125)*

Best **Outdoor Cinema**
★★★ Thission Open-Air Cinema, *7 Apostolou Pavlou St. (p 121)*

Previous page: A performer represents the ancient Greek muse of theater at the opening ceremony of the Athens 2004 Olympic Games.
This page: Ballet choreographed by Maurice Béjart at the Herodes Atticus Theater.

Gazi, Psyrri & Koukaki Arts & Entertainment

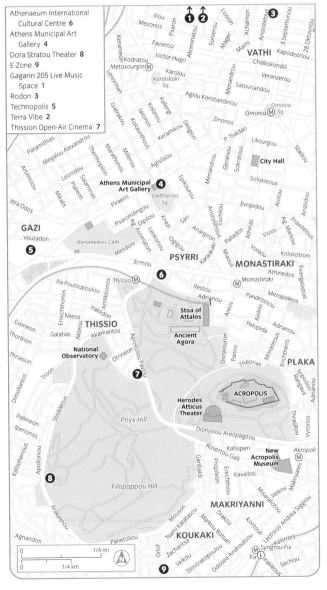

Plaka & Makriyanni Arts & Entertainment

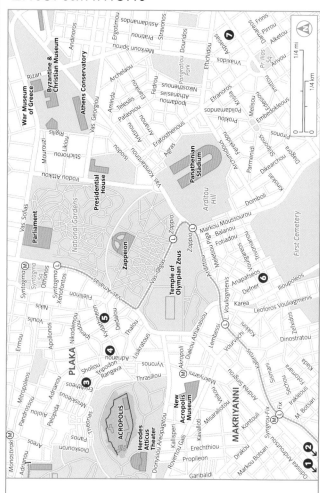

Lycabettus Arts & Entertainment

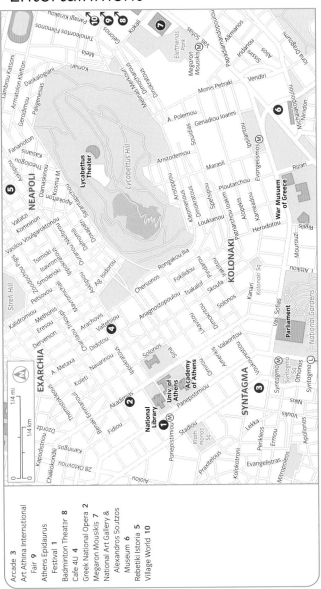

Arcade **3**
Art Athina International Fair **9**
Athens Epidaurus Festival **1**
Badminton Theater **8**
Cafe 4U **4**
Greek National Opera **2**
Megaron Mousikis **7**
National Art Gallery & Alexandros Soutzos Museum **6**
Rebetiki Istoria **5**
Village World **10**

Arts & Entertainment A to Z

Art

Art Athina International Fair

MAROUSSI   The funny, thought-pro-voking, and avant-garde paintings, installations, sculpture, video art, and photography from this fair appear in May at the **Helexpo Palace** exhibition center (☎ 210/616-8888; fax 210/616-8800; www.helexpo.gr), formerly the Olympics press center. *39 Kifissias Ave.* ☎ *210/756-7737. www.art-athina.gr. Metro: Maroussi, then municipal bus: 10. Map p 119.*

Athens Municipal Art Gallery

KOUMOUNDOUROU   This central gallery holds decent temporary exhibits; the main 20th-century Greek artists are all represented here. The collection of works by the architect Ernst Ziller, who designed royal buildings around Athens, is historically and artistically interesting, and includes drawings of the National Theatre, the Municipal Theatre, and private homes. *51 Piraeos St.* ☎ *210/324-3023. Mon–Fri*

9am–1pm & 5–9pm; Sun 9am–1pm. Free admission. Metro: Thissio or Omonia. Map p 117.

Frissiras Museum

PLAKA   This museum of contemporary painting claims to be exclusively dedicated to the human figure, but its exhibits vary. The gallery, spread across two buildings, rotates more than 3,000 works of local and European figure-focused artists. *3 & 7 Monis Asteriou St.* ☎ *210/323-4678. www.frissiras museum.com. Wed–Fri 10am–5pm; Sat–Sun 11am–5pm. Tickets 6€; 3€ seniors, students & groups of 4 or more. Metro: Syntagma. Map p 118.*

National Art Gallery & Alexandros Soutzos Museum

HILTON   Soutzos bequeathed his estate and collection of art to start the city's main art museum. The gallery has Greek and foreign 19th- and 20th-century paintings and curates widely appealing temporary exhibitions. Most paintings are post-

Visitors to the National Art Gallery & Alexandros Soutzos Museum view an exhibition of Colombian artist Fernando Botero.

The ancient Epidaurus outdoor theater in Epidavros can seat 15,000 spectators.

Byzantine, but the Renaissance collection is a valuable addition. *60 Vas. Konstantinou St. ☎ 210/723-5937. www.nationalgallery.gr. Mon & Wed–Sat 9am–3pm; Sun 10am–2pm. Tickets 6.50€; free for 11 & under; 3€ children 12–18. Metro: Evangelismos. Map p 119.*

Cinema

★★★ **Cine Paris** PLAKA   The facade of this open-air, seasonal cinema opposite Plaka's main square is deceiving: The screen is actually in the roof terrace garden. Most movies are in English with Greek subtitles, and there's a bar on-site. For an interesting gift, check out the collection of Greek-language movie posters. *22 Kydathineon St. ☎ 210/ 322-2071. Tickets 7€. Metro: Syntagma. Map p 118.*

★ **kids Planetarium** AMPHITHEA See 1-hour films on a large-format iWerks dome screen on various educational but entertaining subjects (space, the sea, and so on). The IMAX-like films are dazzling when seen from 360 degrees, as they are here. *See p 35, ⑩. Map p 118.*

★★★ **Thission Open-Air Cinema** THISSIO   There are many great outdoor cinemas (see Cine Paris, above), but this popular

garden theater is particularly charming, on the main pedestrian street near the Acropolis, and screens old favorites as well as new ones. Don't be surprised if you can't find a showtime—schedules aren't always posted, though there are usually two screenings, at around 7 to 8pm and 9 to 10pm. *7 Apostolou Pavlou St. ☎ 210/347-0980. Tickets 7€. Metro: Thissio. Map p 117.*

Village World MAROUSSI   At the opposite end of the cultural spectrum, this modern entertainment

The Frissiras Museum occupies two handsome restored neoclassical mansions in Plaka.

complex in the mall has a 14-screen cinema, bowling, an Internet cafe, and a juice bar, but it gets the job done. *35 Andrea Papandreou St.* ☎ *210/610-4100. www.village cinemas.gr. Metro or Proastiakos: Nerantziotissa. Map p 119.*

Classical Music, Opera & Dance

Athenaeum International Cultural Centre THISSIO Ensembles (including opera, baroque, string quartet, choir, and children's choir) perform January to May at this conservatory. The Maria Callas Grand Prix, an international competition offering cash and prizes to performing pianists and vocalists, is also held here. *3 Adrianou St.* ☎ *210/ 321-1987. www.athenaeum.com.gr. Tickets 10€; 5€ students. Metro: Thissio or Monastiraki. Map p 117.*

★★★ Athens Epidaurus Festival PANEPISTIMIOU Ancient drama, opera, symphonies, ballet, and modern dance all appear in Athens at the ancient outdoor **Herodes Atticus Theater** (☎ 210/324-2121 or 210/ 323-2771) and **Lycabettus Theater** (☎ 210/722-7233), and in Epidavros at the ancient **Epidaurus Theater** (☎ 27530/22-026), which you can get to by bus or boat. *Box office: 39 Panepistimiou St.* ☎ *210/327-2000. www.greekfestival.gr. May–Oct. Ticket prices vary. Metro: Panepistimiou. Map p 119.*

★★ Dora Stratou Theater FILOPAPPOU Since 1953, traditional Greek folk dances have been staged here on Filopappou Hill. The Dora Stratou troupe is an institution in Athens, and the outdoor theater is a fitting spot for them. *Box office: 8 Scholiou St.* ☎ *210/324-4395. Theater: Filopappou Hill.* ☎ *210/ 921-4650. www.grdance.org. Performances: May–Sept Tues–Sat 9:30pm; Sun 8:15pm. Ticket office: 9am–4pm; 7:30–9pm before performances. Tickets 15€. Metro: Petralona or bus/trolley: 15, 227. Map p 117.*

Greek National Opera OMONIA From September to June, opera and ballet performances for adults take place at the **Olympia Theatre**, while the **Akropol Theatre** chiefly hosts opera for children. Many festival productions are hosted at the ancient **Herodes Atticus** in summer (see Athens Epidaurus Festival, above). *Olympia Theatre: 59–61 Akademias St.* ☎ *210/364-3725. Akropol: 9–11 Ippokratous St.* ☎ *210/364-3700. www.nationalopera.gr. Box office*

The wood paneling of the acoustically designed Megaron Mousikis concert hall makes for superb listening.

A *Bouzouki* Night

The *bouzouki*, a stringed instrument, is played at many restaurants in the Psyrri and Plaka districts. For a sampling of a few, you can go on an organized tour that includes dinner and dancing. Some of the better-known tour operators are **CHAT Tours,** 4 Stadiou St. (☎ 210/322-3137 or 322-3886), and **Key Tours,** 4 Kallirois St. (☎ 210/923-3166; www.keytours. gr), which both offer "Athens by Night" tours for about 100€ (including dinner). If you venture out on your own, keep in mind that for big *bouzouki* clubs, you need deep pockets, as the norm is sharing a 100€ to 300€ bottle of whiskey with friends while settling in for a long night. Also note that buying baskets of flowers to throw at the songsters has replaced plate smashing.

The bouzouki was the precursor of the lute and is a staple of rebetika music.

daily 9am–9pm. Ticket prices vary. Metro: Omonia. Map p 119.

★ **Megaron Mousikis** EMBASSY The acoustics at this modern concert hall are excellent—that's what it was designed for—as is the classical music program that runs from September to June. *Vas. Sofias & Kokkali sts.* ☎ 210/729-0391 or 210/728-2333. *Central ticket kiosk: 1 Ermou St.* ☎ 210/324-3297. www.megaron.gr. *Box office: Mon–Fri 10am–6pm; Sat 10am–2pm; longer on performance nights, including Sun 6–8:30pm. Kiosk: Mon–Fri 10am–6pm. Tickets 14€–100€. Metro: Megaron Mousikis. Map p 119.*

Dinner Shows

Gialino Music Theatre NEA SMYRNI This show, drink, and dinner venue hosts Greek and foreign acts. It's quite a large operation, and the performances vary from magic to music to dance, such as the Paris Can Can. *143 Syngrou Ave.* ☎ 210/ 931-5600. www.gialino.gr. *Tickets from 20€. Tram: Aigaiou or bus: A2,*

B2, E2, E22, 040, 450, 550, 126 or trolley: 9. Map p 118.

Rebetiki Istoria NEAPOLI For good *rebetika* (the Greek equivalent of jazz, popularized by the underclass in the 1920s and 1930s), this established if smoky club features lively acts and an intellectual crowd. *181 Ippokratous St.* ☎ 210/642-4937. *Sept–Easter Tues–Sun; June Fri–Sat only; closed July–Aug. Cover 6€ includes first drink. Bus: 230. Map p 119.*

★★ **Stamatopoulos** PLAKA The walls of this taverna are painted with murals of Greek revelers characteristic of old Athens. It's a nice touch to go with the good traditional music. *26 Lissiou St. at Flessa St.* ☎ 210/ 322-8722. www.stamatopoulos tavern.gr. *Daily 7pm–2am. Metro: Syntagma. Map 118.*

Internet & Games

Arcade SYNTAGMA This quiet, sparse cybercafe off a main street in Syntagma is an easy place get online. *5 Stadiou St.* ☎ 210/322-1808. *Daily*

The Best Arts & Entertainment

Who's Playing

Comprehensive listings for major music events can be found in magazines such as **Athinorama** (www.athinorama.gr), which is available only in Greek—but you should be able to make out foreign acts if you're clever. Also check the billboards around Monastiraki station (at Ermou St.) or pick up the free listings at boxes outside Metro stations to see what musical acts are in town. If you need more assistance, ask at your hotel or check **www.rockpages.gr** for upcoming pop and rock.

Tickets can be bought through organizers, promoters, venues, ticket agents, and certain record stores, such as **Metropolis,** 64 and 54 Panepistimiou St. (☎ 210/380-8549; www.metropolis.gr), and **Virgin,** 7–9 Stadiou St. (☎ 210/331-4788; www.virginmega.gr). **Ticketnet,** 46 Kifissias Ave. (☎ 210/884-0600; www.ticketnet.gr); **Ticket House,** 42 Panepistimiou St. (☎ 210/360-8366; www.ticket house.gr); and **Ticket Shop** (☎ 210/336-2888; www.ticketshop.gr) also list and sell tickets for Athens venues.

9am–11pm. Minimum charge: 1.80€ for 30 min. Metro: Syntagma. Map p 119.

Cafe 4U EXARCHIA There's a laid-back atmosphere at this 24-hour Internet cafe that sells food and drinks (at the bar). In addition to Web access, there are board games and several TVs. 44 Ippokratous St. ☎ 210/361-1981. www.cafe4u.gr. Metro: Omonia. Map p 119.

The Half Note Jazz Club, across from the First Cemetery, has been around for more than 30 years.

E-Zone KOUKAKI The i-addicted can play games, check e-mail, and copy CDs or DVDs here. It's open 24 hours, with vending coffee and snacks. Veikou & Orlof sts. ☎ 210/922-0431. Minimum charge: 1.50€. Metro: Syngrou-Fix or trolley: 1, 5, 15. Map p 117.

Jazz Music
Half Note Jazz Club METS
The Half Note has hosted jazz majors and minors from across the pond for 30 years, but it still feels fresh. This is where to go for jazz, period. 17 Trivonianou St. ☎ 210/921-3310. www.halfnote.gr. Tues–Sat 10:30pm till late; Sun–Mon 8:30pm till late. Tickets: 30€ including first drink; tables 35€ or 40€. Bus: A3, B3, 057. Map p 118.

Popular Music
Gagarin 205 Live Music Space
THYMARAKIA Standing 1,300 or seating 600, this is no small music club. The hall is a little out of the way, but regularly hosts big live

The Olympic Equestrian Center, adjacent to the Athens Race Track (see p 126) in Markopolou, has 300 stables, an hanger-sized indoor school, and a cross-country course.

foreign acts, such as Morrissey and Godspeed You Black Emperor. *205 Liosion Ave.* ☎ *210/854-7601. www. gagarin205.gr. Metro: Attikis. Map p 117.*

Rodon OMONIA   The Rodon is another spot to see local and foreign acts that have made it to the pop charts, and it's one of the oldest in town. In fact, it basically introduced world rock and pop to Athens in the 1970s. *24 Marni St.* ☎ *210/524-7427. Metro: Omonia. Map p 117.*

★★ **kids Technopolis** GAZI   The attractive grounds of the old Athens gasworks are now venues for concerts (among other things, such as art exhibits) in this trendiest of

areas. The chimneys, cauldrons, and funnels can make a concert an interesting experience. *100 Piraeos St. at Persefonis St.* ☎ *210/346-1589 or 210/346-7322. Metro: Kerameikos. Map p 117.*

Terra Vibe MALAKASA   This outdoor park for big-name pop and rock acts opened in 2004. The well-known multiday Rockwave Festival there has street theater, extreme sports, art exhibitions, and, of course, a slew of famous musicians. Shuttle buses bring the crowds. *Lamia National Rd. at Malakasa junction.* ☎ *210/882-0426. www.didi music.gr. Tickets: www.tickethouse. gr. Tickets from 40€. Train: Sfendali Station. Map p 117.*

Greek Drama

Athenians loved theater in antiquity—in fact, they practically invented comedy, tragedy, and satire—and today they still do. Many small theatrical productions in native Greek are still staged for adults and children throughout Athens in local playhouses. For this authentic experience, consult a listings magazine like **Athinorama** (in Greek), or try **www.ellthea.gr**, which summarizes plots and gives practical info for some venues. Tickets are around 20€.

For the Sports Fan

The Greeks are fiercely devoted to sport, with soccer and basketball holding a special place in Athenian hearts. Many professional clubs throughout Greece have teams for multiple sports, the biggest among them eternal enemies **Panathinaikos FC** (☎ 801/111-1908; www.ticketclub.gr) and **Olympiakos Piraeus** (☎ 210/414-3000; www.olympiakos.gr). These two teams often meet at Olympiakos's **Karaiskaki Stadium** (☎ 210/480-0900; www.karaiskaki.gr) to compete in soccer, and the rivalry is intense. **AEK,** another club, also plays in Athens at the distinctive Calatrava-designed **Olympic Athletic Center of Athens** (☎ 210/683-4060; www.oaka.com.gr).

If they're not watching sports, you can be sure Greeks are betting on them. The **Athens Race Track** at Markopolou (☎ 22990/81-000) is a good spot to get a taste of this. Here you can spend a day at the horse races (minimum bet: 1.50€), with free coffee, snacks, and bus transport from Koropi Station every half-hour from 3:15pm.

If you're more the solitary type, the Athens coast has a nice **golf course in Glyfada,** at Terma Pronois Street (☎ 210/894-6820; www.golfglyfada.com). Rent clubs (20€), drive balls (14€), play tennis (16€ per hour), or head out to the greens (from 42€) at this challenging 18-hole resort. Of course, if you're with a local, there might be money on that, too.

Emiliano Moretti of Italy (below left) battles Mauro Rosales of Argentina for a ball in the 2004 Olympic soccer semi-finals in Karaiskaki Stadium.

Theater

★ kids Badminton Theater

GOUDI   This 2,500-seat former Olympic venue (formerly used for badminton, obviously) was converted in 2007 and hosts a variety of family entertainment shows, such as *Mamma Mia!* and *Cats. Kannelopoulou Ave.* ☎ *211/101-0020. www.badmintontheater.gr. Tickets: www.ticketnet.gr. Ticket prices vary. Metro: Katehaki. Map p 119.*

kids Coronet Theatre PANGRATI

This wintertime venue hosts a variety of live acts appealing to international audiences of all ages, including traveling Broadway musicals, magic shows, and children's plays. *11 Frinis St. at Imittou St.* ☎ *210/701-2123. www.coronet.gr. Sept–May. Tickets 15€–25€. Trolley: 4, 11. Map p 118.* ●

Lodging **Best Bets**

The pool at the Athenaeum Intercontinental operates from May through September, weather permitting.

Best **Quiet Hotel Near the Acropolis**
Acropolis View Hotel $ *10 Webster St. (p 132)*

Best **Supersize Luxury Hotel**
Athenaeum Intercontinental $$$ *89–93 Syngrou Ave. (p 133)*

Best **Hostel**
★★ Athens Backpackers $ *12 Makri St. (p 133)*

Best **Budget Lodging for Families**
★★★ Athens Studios $ *3A Veikou St. (p 134)*

Best **Hotel with Conveniently Located Parking**
★ Central Athens Hotel $$ *21 Apollonos St. (p 134)*

Best **All-Rounder**
★★★ Electra Palace $$$ *18 Nikodimou St. (p 135)*

Best **Trendy Hotel**
Fresh Hotel $$ *26 Sofokleous St. (p 135)*

Best **Old-World Luxury Hotel**
★★★ Grande Bretagne $$$$ *Syntagma Sq. (p 136)*

Best **Midsize Hotel Near the Acropolis**
★★ Herodion Hotel $$ *4 Rovertou Galli St. (p 136)*

Best **Modern Luxury Hotel**
★ Hilton Athens $$$$ *46 Vas. Sofias Ave. (p 136)*

Best **Conveniently Located Budget Hotels**
★ Hotel Attalos $ *29 Athinas St. (p 136)*; and ★ Adonis Hotel $ *3 Kodrou St. (p 132)*

Best **Boutique Hotel**
★ Ochre & Brown $$$ *7 Leokoriou St. (p 137)*

Previous page: The Winter Garden, a cafe in the lobby of the Grande Bretagne, has an elegant stained-glass ceiling.

Makriyanni & Koukaki Lodging

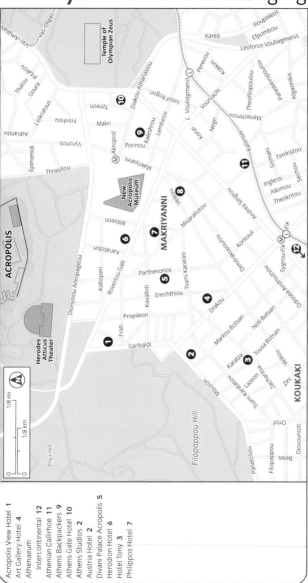

Acropolis View Hotel **1**
Art Gallery Hotel **4**
Athenaeum
Intercontinental **12**
Athenian Callirhoe **11**
Athens Backpackers **9**
Athens Gate Hotel **10**
Athens Studios **2**
Austria Hotel **2**
Divani Palace Acropolis **5**
Herodion Hotel **6**
Hotel Tony **3**
Philippos Hotel **7**

Psyrri, Monastiraki & Plaka Lodging

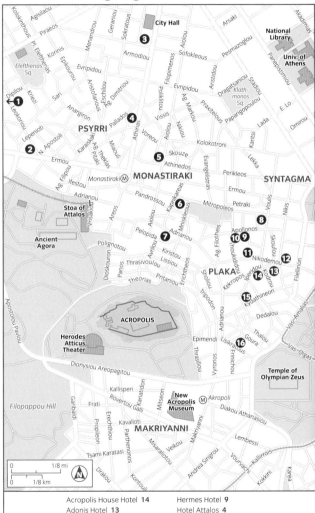

Acropolis House Hotel 14
Adonis Hotel 13
Adrian Hotel 7
Amazon Hotel 8
Ava Hotel 16
Central Athens Hotel 10
Electra Palace 11
Fresh Hotel 3

Hermes Hotel 9
Hotel Attalos 4
Hotel Plaka 6
Jason Inn 1
Niki Hotel 12
Ochre & Brown 2
Student & Travellers Inn 15
Tempi Hotel 5

Syntagma & Kolonaki
Lodging

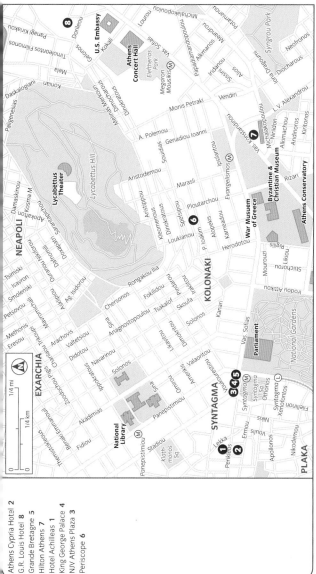

Athens Cypria Hotel **2**
G.R. Louis Hotel **8**
Grande Bretagne **5**
Hilton Athens **7**
Hotel Achilleas **1**
King George Palace **4**
NJV Athens Plaza **3**
Periscope **6**

Athens Lodging A to Z

Acropolis House Hotel PLAKA
This is a popular budget hotel in a restored 150-year-old villa on a quiet pedestrian street that straddles Syntagma and Plaka. Stick to the old wing, with its classical architecture. Rooms without air-conditioning are cheaper. *6–8 Kodrou St.* ☎ *210/322-2344. www.acropolishouse.gr. 25 units. Doubles 50€–87€ w/breakfast. MC, V only to reserve (pay in cash). Metro: Syntagma. Map p 130.*

Acropolis View Hotel KOUKAKI
On a quiet side street close to the Acropolis in a bedroom neighborhood, it has small, clean rooms, some with balconies facing the Parthenon (such as no. 407), as well as a roof terrace. *10 Webster St. at Rovertou Galli St.* ☎ *210/921-7303 or 210/921-7305. www.acropolisview.gr. 32 units. Doubles 80€–100€ w/breakfast. MC, V. Metro: Akropoli or Syngrou-Fix or bus/trolley: 1, 5, 15, 230. Map p 129.*

The simple unadorned roof of the Adonis Hotel has a charming view of backstreet Plaka houses and the Acropolis.

★ **Adonis Hotel** PLAKA   This value-for-money hotel in a great location near the shopping district and Syntagma Square on a quiet street has Spartan rooms, some with big balconies. The rooftop cafe (good for breakfast) has an Acropolis view. *3 Kodrou St.* ☎ *210/324-9737. www.hotel-adonis.gr. 26 units. Doubles 62€–92€ w/breakfast. No credit cards, except to reserve. Metro: Syntagma. Map p 130.*

★ **Adrian Hotel** PLAKA   Kitty-corner to a cafe-lined square on Plaka's main pedestrian street, you can have breakfast and lounge in the Acropolis-view roof garden, or on one of the room balconies. *74 Adrianou St.* ☎ *210/322-1553. www.douros-hotels.com. 22 units. Doubles 82€–150€ w/breakfast. MC, V. Metro: Monastiraki. Map p 130.*

Amazon Hotel SYNTAGMA
An easy-access location on a street straddling Plaka and the pedestrian shopping district, this basic hotel has some roomy doubles. *19 Mitropoleos & 7 Pendelis sts.* ☎ *210/323-4002 and 210/323-4005. www.amazonhotel.gr. 46 units. Doubles 80€–111€ w/breakfast. AE, DC, MC, V. Metro: Syntagma. Map p 130.*

★ **kids Art Gallery Hotel** KOUKAKI   This clean, simple, and friendly circa-1950s converted house, former home to an artist, maintains an artistic flair with spacious rooms (by European standards), old-fashioned radiators, and hardwood floors in a convenient Athenian neighborhood. *5 Erechthiou St.* ☎ *210/923-8376. www.artgalleryhotel.gr. 21 units. Doubles 70€–100€. No credit cards. Metro: Syngrou-Fix or bus/trolley: 1, 5, 15, 230. Map p 129.*

kids **Athenaeum Intercontinental** NEOS KOSMOS When only no-fuss, American-sized luxury will do (Bill Clinton stayed here). Athens's biggest luxe hotel is efficient and has large rooms, a 24-hour restaurant, a pool, a spa, and a nearby cinema complex. It's a 15-minute walk from the city center. *89–93 Syngrou Ave.* ☎ *210/920-6000. www.intercontinental.com. 543 units. Doubles 230€–260€. AE, DC, MC, V. Metro: Syngrou-Fix or bus/trolley: 9, A2, B2, E2, E22, 040, 450, 550, 126 or tram: Neos Kosmos. Map p 129.*

Athenian Callirhoe MAKRIYANNI A beautifully appointed modern midsize boutique hotel, it's near all the main sites, though on a very busy corner. The rooftop dining with an Acropolis view and the sauna are both elegant. *32 Kallirois Ave.* ☎ *210/921-5353. www.tac.gr. 84 units. Doubles 150€ w/breakfast. AE, DC, MC, V. Metro: Akropoli or tram: Fix. Map p 129.*

★★ Athens Backpackers MAKRIYANNI This always-full, bunk bed hostel organizes tours

The Athenaeum Intercontinental atrium is dominated by Electromagnetic Sphere, *a sculpture by Greek artist Takis.*

and BBQs. It's lively and the staff is friendly. The rooftop bar has an Acropolis view. *12 Makri St.* ☎ *210/922-4044. www.back packers.gr. 60 units. Price per bed: 18€–25€. MC, V. Metro: Akropoli. Map p 129.*

Lodging Tips

Athens is a tourist town awash with hotels. There are countless good ones, particularly in the historic center around the Acropolis, where most tourists stay (encompassing the neighborhoods of Syntagma, Plaka, Monastiraki, Thissio, Makriyanni, and Koukaki). Many of these hotels have also been renovated in the past 10 years, part of a splurge to update Athens for the 2004 Olympics. To find particularly good deals in post-Olympic upgraded hotels, book online or ask about off-the-rack-rate rooms during the off season (often July and Aug), for multiple-night stays, or with cash payment. Hotels outside the center of town may also be a bargain, especially since the efficient Metro (another Olympics-related development project) runs all over town. Finally, hotels can request an advance payment of up to 25% of the total for a multiple-night stay, or not less than 1 night's rate, and some may accept cash only.

The lobby level of the Electra Palace also features a restaurant, Motivo, and the Duck Tail Bar.

Athens Cypria Hotel SYNTAGMA This is a popular business hotel—and thus is relatively empty during the low season of July and August—on a narrow street with outdoor cafes just 3 blocks from Syntagma Square. It's cheerful, too, with bright white walls. Room nos. 603 to 607 overlook the Acropolis. Book ahead. *5 Diomias St.* ☎ *210/323-8034 or 210/323-0470. www.athenscypria. com. 115 units. Doubles 119€–129€ w/breakfast. AE, MC, V. Metro: Syntagma. Map p 131.*

Athens Gate Hotel MAKRIYANNI A central location on a busy street, clean rooms, top-notch service, and the rooftop breakfast and restaurant with superb views make this a solid choice for couples or older travelers. *10 Syngrou Ave.* ☎ *210/923-8302. www.athensgate.gr. 99 units. Doubles 100€–130€ w/breakfast. AE, DC, MC, V. Metro: Akropoli. Map p 129.*

★★★ kids Athens Studios MAKRIYANNI Backpackers often upgrade from the Backpackers hostel (see p 133) to these Ikea-kitted, self-catering apartments, also ideal for families. There is a sports bar and a self-service laundry downstairs. *3A Veikou St.* ☎ *210/923-5811. www.athensstudios.gr. 35 units. Apt for 2–3 people 70€–120€. MC, V. Metro: Akropoli. Map p 129.*

Austria Hotel KOUKAKI Get a great rooftop view of the city, the Parthenon, and even the islands at this well-maintained if Spartan hotel on the road to the Dora Stratou Theater, practically around the corner from the Acropolis. *7 Mousson St.* ☎ *210/923-5151. www.austria hotel.com. 37 units. Doubles 60€–90€ w/breakfast. AE, DC, MC, V. Metro: Syngrou-Fix or bus: 230. Map p 129.*

★ kids Ava Hotel PLAKA Ava's spacious, clean, and comfortable studios with kitchenettes, on a quiet street in the old town, are great for families and businesspeople staying in Athens for a while. Check with the hotel for special offers. *9–11 Lyssikratous St.* ☎ *210/325-9000. www.avahotel.gr. 15 units. 111€–308€ w/breakfast. AE, MC, V. Metro: Akropoli. Map p 130.*

★ Central Athens Hotel SYNTAGMA Modern furnishings,

attentive service, perfect location: This midprice hotel hits all its marks. Twin rooms at the back have an Acropolis view, while bigger front rooms have balconies and king-size beds. There's also a rooftop lounge and parking. *21 Apollonos St.* ☎ *210/323-4357. www.central hotel.gr. 84 units. Doubles 99€– 121€ w/breakfast. AE, DC, MC, V. Metro: Syntagma. Map p 130.*

Divani Palace Acropolis

MAKRIYANNI   This large anchor hotel is in a quiet residential neighborhood, though it caters mainly to tour groups. It has an outdoor pool and a rooftop restaurant (with an extensive breakfast buffet), and rooms are big if bland, with balconies. *19–25 Parthenonos St.* ☎ *210/928-0100. www.divanis.gr. 253 units. Doubles 143€–440€ w/breakfast. AE, DC, MC, V. Metro: Syngrou-Fix. Map p 129.*

★★★ Electra Palace PLAKA   The

luxury Electra is the biggest hotel in Plaka. Higher floors here have smaller rooms but bigger balconies—in fact, you'll want to stick to the top floor, well off the street and with an Acropolis view. Amenities include indoor and outdoor pools, a gym, and a steam room. *18 Nikodimou St.* ☎ *210/324-1401 or 210/337-0000.*

The Air Lounge roof bar at Fresh Hotel serves coffee, light lunch, finger food, dinner, and cocktails.

www.electrahotels.gr. 150 units. Doubles 180€–360€ w/breakfast. AE, DC, MC, V. Metro: Syntagma. Map p 130.

Fresh Hotel OMONIA   A designer boutique hotel all Perspex and pastels, with a rooftop pool, it attracts the young and hip (good marketing?), but is located in one of the city's grittiest areas, which I otherwise wouldn't recommend for visiting friends or relatives. *26 Sofokleous St. at Kleisthenous St.* ☎ *210/524-8511. www.freshhotel.gr. 133 units. Doubles 155€–175€ w/breakfast. AE, DC, MC, V. Metro: Omonia. Map p 130.*

The beaux-arts lobby of the Grande Bretagne has vaulted ceilings, mosaic floors, and Persian carpets.

★★★ **Grande Bretagne** SYN-TAGMA   This plush 160-year-old landmark hotel, now part of the Starwood Luxury Collection, has an Acropolis-view rooftop bar-restaurant, a super spa, an indoor pool, and an outdoor rooftop pool, not to mention incredible service, beautiful rooms, and a lobby bar. *Syntagma Sq.* ☎ *210/333-0000. www.grande bretagne.gr. 321 units. Doubles 317€–611€. AE, DC, MC, V. Metro: Syntagma. Map p 131.*

G. R. Louis Hotel EMBASSY   The boutique hotel in the business district has big, opulent rooms and rich decor. A lively restaurant-bar area is at nearby Alexandras Avenue and Mavili Square, and it's 2 blocks from the U.S. embassy if you get into trouble. *22 Timoleontos Vassou St.* ☎ *210/641-5000. www.grlouis.gr. 31 units. Doubles 130€. AE, DC, MC, V. Metro: Ambelokipi or bus/trolley: A5, E6, E7, G5, X14, X95, 3, 7, 8, 13, 022, 060, 408. Map p 131.*

★ **Hermes Hotel** SYNTAGMA   This renovated well-kept hotel has spacious rooms (by city standards) and marble bathrooms, and is on a quiet street in a perfect location.

Guest rooms at the Hilton Athens have high-speed Internet, mountain or Acropolis views, and marble bathrooms with a bathtub and walk-in shower.

19 Apollonos St. ☎ *210/323-5514 or 210/322-2706. www.hermeshotel.gr. 45 units. Doubles 95€–150€ w/breakfast. AE, DC, MC, V. Metro: Syntagma. Map p 130.*

★★ **Herodion Hotel** MAKRIYANNI   This attractive modern midsize hotel in a leafy neighborhood close to the Acropolis has helpful staff and a rooftop Jacuzzi. The rooms are large. *4 Rovertou Galli St.* ☎ *210/ 923-6832. www.herodion.gr. 90 units. Doubles 130€–250€. AE, DC, MC, V. Metro: Akropoli. Map p 129.*

★ **Hilton Athens** HILTON   Athens's iconic 1963 landmark luxe hotel on the point between two arterial roads has an indoor and outdoor pool and spa and is one of the most recognizable buildings in the city. The facade artwork is by "Generation of the '30s" artist Yiannis Moralis. *46 Vas. Sofias Ave.* ☎ *210/728-1000. www.athens.hilton.com. 523 units. Doubles 217€–428€ w/breakfast. AE, DC, MC, V. Metro: Evangelismos. Map p 131.*

Hotel Achilleas SYNTAGMA   You can't go wrong at this renovated business hotel with minimalist decor and a helpful staff on a quiet street close to Syntagma Square in the main shopping area. If you can get a room, that is—it's a popular choice for the location and price. *21 Lekka St.* ☎ *210/323-3197. www.achilleas hotel.gr. 34 units. Doubles 80€– 135€ w/breakfast. AE, MC, V. Metro: Syntagma. Map p 131.*

★ **Hotel Attalos** MONASTIRAKI   This is a very popular budget hotel located on lively Athinas Street. There's a roof-terrace snack bar as well as Acropolis-view rooms. *29 Athinas St.* ☎ *210/321-2801. www.attaloshotel.com. 80 units. Doubles 60€–94€; 10% discount for Frommer's readers. AE, MC, V. Metro: Monastiraki. Map p 130.*

Hotel Plaka MONASTIRAKI   The rooms at this convenient hotel close to Monastiraki station seem small, but this place is popular. Request an Acropolis view. *7 Kapnikareas St. at Mitropoleos St.* ☎ *210/322-2096. www.plakahotel.gr. 67 units. Doubles 95€–145€ w/breakfast. AE, DC, MC, V. Metro: Monastiraki or bus: 025, 026, 027. Map p 130.*

kids **Hotel Tony** KOUKAKI   A pink building on a residential street, Tony's is a budget hotel in a bedroom neighborhood. Self-contained studios will suit families or longer stays, and there's a communal kitchen. *26 Zacharitsa St.* ☎ *210/ 923-0561 or 210/923-5761. www. hoteltony.gr. 21 units. Doubles 60€. No credit cards. Metro: Syngrou-Fix or trolley: 1, 5, 15. Map p 129.*

Jason Inn PSYRRI   You can Acropolis-gaze from the roof garden over breakfast at this moderate hotel that's on the edge of trendy Psyrri, Thissio, and Monastiraki, with their restaurants, bars, and sidewalk cafes, and a short walk to even trendier Gazi. *12 Agion Asomaton St.* ☎ *210/ 325-1106. Reservations* ☎ *210/520-2491. www.douros-hotels.com. 57 units. Doubles 70€–95€ w/breakfast. MC, V. Metro: Thissio. Map p 130.*

★ **King George Palace** SYNTAGMA   This modern hotel in the most central part of town has a comfy lounge-bar-restaurant, an indoor pool and sauna, and a gorgeous Acropolis view from the restaurant, where you can enjoy a quiet midday coffee. *3 Vas. Georgiou St.* ☎ *210/322-2210. www.classical hotels.com. 78 units. Doubles 320€– 740€. Metro: Syntagma. Map p 131.*

Niki Hotel PLAKA   This hotel on a quiet, convenient, and trendy street has small rooms and bathrooms, but this is Europe. Higher floors have balconies and there's a bar-lounge downstairs. *27 Nikis St.* ☎ *210/322-0913. www.nikihotel.gr. 23 units. Doubles 80€–107€ w/breakfast. AE, MC, V. Metro: Syntagma. Map p 130.*

kids **NJV Athens Plaza** SYNTAGMA   Located at the most central (and busy) yet convenient part of town, this large, bustling hotel is run by a family-friendly chain. *Syntagma Sq.* ☎ *210/335-2400. www.classicalhotels.com. 182 units. Doubles 440€ w/breakfast. AE, DC, MC, V. Metro: Syntagma. Map p 131.*

★ **Ochre & Brown** PSYRRI   When you stay at this minimalist,

A plush double room at the King George Palace, which has been home to heads of state and celebrities since 1936.

plush boutique hotel on an otherwise quiet street in the bar and restaurant district, be sure to enjoy an Athens night out in the neighborhood. *7 Leokoriou St.* 210/331-2950. www.oandbhotel.com. *11 units. Doubles 145€–280€ w/breakfast. AE, MC, V. Metro: Thissio or Monastiraki. Map p 130.*

★ **Periscope** KOLONAKI You can designer-shop, stroll, party, and then sleep at this minimalist (including space), subtly nautical hotel in the most chichi Athens district. *22 Haritos St.* 210/729-7200. www.periscope.gr. *21 units. Doubles 160€ w/breakfast. AE, DC, MC, V & debit cards. Metro: Syntagma or bus: 022, 060, 200. Map p 131.*

Philippos Hotel MAKRIYANNI The sister hotel of the Herodion around the corner has more of a boutique feel, with sleek polished wood. The landing is midstairwell, so not for those with mobility

issues. *3 Mitseon St.* 210/922-3611. www.philipposhotel.gr. *50 units. Doubles 85€–140€. AE, DC, MC, V. Metro: Akropoli. Map p 129.*

Student & Travellers Inn PLAKA Though a bit more expensive than other hostels (but certainly not a "hotel"), the location in the real "heart of Athens" is advertisement enough. A family room is available. *16 Kydathineon St.* 210/324-4808. www.hihostels.com. *25 units (61 beds). Doubles from 42€ shared facilities; 70€ private. No credit cards. Metro: Syntagma. Map p 130.*

Tempi Hotel MONASTIRAKI This very popular budget hotel on a pedestrian street facing "flower market" square is also very sparse, very friendly, and very clean, with communal kitchen facilities. *29 Aiolou St.* 210/321-3175. www.tempihotel.gr. *24 units. Doubles 45€–64€. AE, MC, V. Metro: Monastiraki. Map p 130.* ●

Ochre & Brown has only 11 rooms, so you may get to know the other guests at the bar of its BaRestaurant.

The **Argo-Saronic Islands**

Aegina **1**
Hydra **3**
Poros **2**

····· Ferry route

Previous page: Remains of Delphi, on the southwest slopes of Mount Parnassus.

The Argo-Saronic island group, in the adjoining Saronic and Argolic gulfs of the Aegean, is the closest cluster of Greek islands to Athens, and can make an excellent side trip from the city. The easiest way to see the islands is an organized **three-island cruise** to Aegina, Poros, and Hydra, for 93€ with lunch on board, but you can also go on your own: Hydrofoils frequently ply a route stopping at Aegina, Angistri, Poros, Methana, Hydra, Spetses, and Porto Heli. See **www.gtp.gr** and **www.openseas.gr** for sailings from Athens's port of Piraeus. START: **Metro to Piraeus.**

1 Aegina. The island most easily seen from Athens (about 28km/17 miles away) is known for its pistachios. Aegina is the biggest of the group and its town has a pretty 19th-century harbor. Most tourists make a stop at the Doric **Temple of Aphaia** and the **Agios Nektarios** monastery. The port of **Agia Marina** on the east coast is a busy beach resort (though without much of a beach). Make your way past nicer beaches to picturesque **Perdika** (10km/6¼ miles from Agia Marina), a fishing village with seafood tavernas. ⏱ *30–70 min. Summer: Hydrofoil or catamaran every half-hour, car ferry hourly; reduced winter schedule.*

2 Poros. This green enclave (57km/35 miles from Athens) is often crowded by weekending Athenians, especially in July and August, but its cheery beaches can be a fun place for watersports-loving teens. (To add some seriousness, Henry Miller stayed here once, as described in his "Colossus of Marousi.") Separated at its narrowest point from the mainland by 150 to 350m (492–1,148 ft.), a frequent ferry closes the distance. The ancient site of **Trizina** is worth a look, as is the monastery of **Zoodochos Pigi** ("Source of Life"), with its curative springs. Athenian orator Demosthenes (a dissident on the run from the Macedonian king of Athens) is believed to be buried in the courtyard. ⏱ *1 hr. hydrofoil, 2½ hr. car ferry. Summer: Hydrofoil every half-hour, car ferry hourly; reduced winter schedule.*

3 ★★ Hydra. Celebrated by writers and artists, the tumble of cubist, neoclassical *archontika* (mansions) at the port (68km/42 miles) painted in browns—instead of the more familiar humble whitewash of the Cycladic islands—is favored by old Athenian families and publicity-shy celebrities. Even in summer, when throngs of Greeks flock to the beaches, the side streets in **Hydra town** remain quiet. The island's independence flag makes a colorful souvenir. No cars allowed. ⏱ *1½ hr. hydrofoil. Summer: Hydrofoil every half-hour; reduced winter schedule.*

An alley in the fishing village of Poros, on the island of Poros, which has been inhabited since the Bronze Age.

Delphi

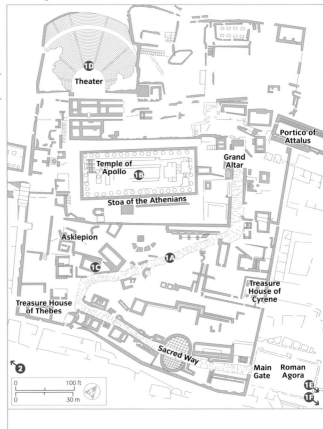

- Theater — **1D**
- Portico of Attalus
- Grand Altar
- Temple of Apollo — **1B**
- Stoa of the Athenians
- Asklepion
- **1C**
- **1A**
- Treasure House of Cyrene
- Treasure House of Thebes
- Sacred Way
- Main Gate
- Roman Agora — **1E** **1F**
- **2**

0	100 ft
0	30 m

GREECE

Delphi
Athens

Aegean Sea

- **1A** Sacred Way
- **1B** Temple of Apollo
- **1C** Athenian Treasury
- **1D** Theater
- **1E** Stadium
- **1F** Tholos Temple
- **2** Archaeological Museum

Visitors to Athens must take a side trip to Delphi if they have time. This "goose bump" site has it all: spectacular ancient remains, a superb museum, and a panoramic setting on Mount Parnassus, with views down to the Gulf of Corinth. Delphi (180km/112 miles from central Athens) can be seen in a day—or, at the least, 3 hours—though that might not be enough time to appreciate it. The best time to visit is in spring, when there are both snow and wildflowers on Parnassus—and relatively few tourists about. START: **Athens Bus Terminal B.**

1 ★★ **Ruins at Delphi.** This is the one of the best archaeological excavations in Greece, and it shows. Some 1,000 years before Apollo was worshiped here, before an oracle advised pilgrims here, or before the Pythian Games were held here, it was called Pytho, a Mycenaean sanctuary of the earth goddess Gaia guarded by her daughter, Python. (That's one version of the story, at least.) It was rededicated in the 4th to 6th centuries B.C. to Apollo Delphi ("Apollo by Dolphin" or "of Delphi"), who was the preeminent oracle of the classical Greek world, and people came from all over Greece to hear his prophesies channeled through high priestesses, called Pythia. In the inner sanctum of the sanctuary at Delphi was the *omphalos,* a special hollow stone believed to channel communication between the oracle and the god, perhaps through vapors, and an eternal flame. Also on the site was the **1A** **Sacred Way path** to the **1B** **Temple of Apollo,** lined with city-state treasuries that tried to outdo each other by offering the greatest riches to the god. The **1C** **Athenian Treasury** looks the best preserved because it was reconstructed in 1906. The 4th-century-B.C. **1D** **theater** on-site is also well preserved, aided by the Romans, who rebuilt it 2,000 years ago. Musicians and performers competed there every 4 years in the Pythian Games held in honor of Apollo, god of poets and inventor of the lyre. These games emphasized culture over athletics, the latter of which took place in a 5th-century-B.C. **1E** **stadium** (redone in the 2nd century A.D.) farther up the hill. Some 800m (½ mile) away is the poster child of Delphi, the 380 B.C. **1F** **Tholos temple,** partially (and very photogenically) reerected

The Doric remains of the Temple of Apollo at Delphi date to the 4th century B.C.

Getting There

Getting to Delphi is relatively easy, as there are usually a few buses daily from the Athens regional Bus Terminal B at 260 Liossion St. (Once in Delphi, you should do all your exploring on foot.) **KTEL buses** (☎ 210/880-8080 or 210/831-7096 in Athens; 226/508-2317 in Delphi) leave six times a day from Athens and take about 3 hours each way. Tickets are 13€. For a guided tour, try **GO tours,** 31–33 Voulis St. (☎ 210/322-5951), or **CHAT tours,** 4 Stadiou St. (☎ 210/322-3137), which offer 1- and 2-day trips that leave Athens by 8am and arrive at Delphi by 3pm. (Take the 2-day tour for a more relaxing time—about 150€ including transportation, all admission fees, guide, hotel, and most meals.) For more information, go to the Delphi town hall tourism office, 12 Frederikis and 11 Apollonos sts. (☎ 226/508-2900), from 7:30am to 2:30pm.

in 1938. 🕘 *3 hr.* ☎ *226/508-2312. www.culture.gr. Admission 6€; 9€ for site & museum. May–Oct Tues–Sun 7:30am–7:15pm, Mon noon–6:30pm; Nov–Apr & some holidays 8:30am–3pm; closed Jan 1, Mar 25, Easter Sunday, Ayiou Pnevmatos (Whit Monday), May 1 & Dec 25–26.*

② ★★ **Archaeological Museum.** Many important finds from the site dating back to the 8th century B.C. are featured in this museum, including *kouri* (stylized statues of youths) from the 7th century B.C. and gifts that were once part of the Sacred Way's treasuries. The beautiful Egyptian-inspired **Naxos sphinx** and the statue of a 474-B.C. Pythian Games

A statue of Agias, a Thessalonian prince and accomplished boxer, at the Archaeological Museum at Delphi.

winner, the bronze **Charioteer of Delphi,** are other standouts. The museum also contains an **omphalos,** or "Navel Stone," an engraved hollow rock shaped like a beehive that marked the center of the world (not to be confused with the original Delphi *omphalos*): Zeus was said to have released two eagles which flew around the world from opposite ends; where they collided and fell to earth marked the center— Delphi. 🕘 *1 hr.* ☎ *226/508-2312. www.culture.gr. Tickets 6€; 9€ museum & site. May–Oct Tues–Sun 7:30am–7:15pm, Mon noon–6:30pm; Nov–Apr & some holidays 8:30am–3pm; closed Jan 1, Mar 25, Easter Sunday, Ayiou Pnevmatos (Whit Monday), May 1 & Dec 25–26.*

Sounion

Temple of Poseidon 1

The temple at Cape Sounion, a promontory at the southern
tip of the Attica peninsula, can be a half-day trip from Athens. It's
high up on most tourists' lists, so avoid weekends and peak hours
(typically sunset—which is beautiful but crowded). The views are
spectacular and served as a strategic watch point for guarding the
Saronic Gulf, and the craggy hills bloom with wildflowers. START:
Athens Bus Terminal B.

---

① ★ Temple of Poseidon. The
majestic 5th-century-B.C. Temple of
Poseidon (6.1m/20-ft. columns are all
that remain) is where mythical King
Aegeus waited for his son, Theseus,
to return from slaying the Cretan
Minotaur. A white sail on Theseus's
ship meant he lived, a black one
meant he had died. But Theseus for-
got to change the sail on his return
journey; the surrounding Aegean Sea
was named for Aegeus when he
jumped from the cliff in sorrow. An
organized tour (35€) will give you
similar information. Go it alone

instead for less money: Buses leave
from central Athens, and once in
Sounion, you can take a cab to the
temple or walk the 1km (⅔ mile) from
the bus stop. Driving by car can be
troublesome, with heavy traffic in
both directions. 🕐 *5 hr. Bus: 2 hr.
(69km/43 miles). KTEL bus station:
Patission St. at Aigyptou Sq. (Stops
at Klathmonos Sq. on Stadiou St. &
beginning of Syngrou Ave.)* 📞 *210/
880-8080. www.ktelattikis.gr. Buses
leave Athens hourly 6:40am–5:30pm;
leave Sounion 8am–7pm winter,
8am–9pm summer. Tickets 5.40€.*

Epidaurus

Theater at Epidaurus 1

····· Ferry route

The ruins of Epidaurus, a small city in ancient Greece on the Saronic Gulf, are now surrounded by the modern town of Epidavros. Epidaurus was purported to be the birthplace of Asklepios, god of healing, and the Asklepion (a temple to the patron god) there flourished as a curative spa in classical times. The city prospered as a result and embarked on several major municipal projects, constructing a huge namesake theater, a banquet hall, baths, and a palaestra. Only a few of these remain. START: **Athens Bus Terminal B.**

❶ ★★ Theater at Epidaurus.

Famous for its acoustics, the 4th-century-B.C. theater is impressive, and can still host up to 14,000 spectators (for mainly ancient Greek plays). Unlike many of the ruins, including the Asklepion, the theater was not pillaged for building blocks in antiquity. As a result, it is astonishingly well preserved; restorations have been both minimal and tactful. From the nosebleed section over 55 rows away, you can still hear a whisper onstage. Also on the site are an **excavation museum** and the **Epidaurus Festival Museum,** as well as the scant remains of the **sanctuary of Asklepios.** (If visiting the Asklepion sanctuary, visit the excavation museum first to get an idea of the original ancient layout.) The real draw here, though, is the theater. 🕐 *6-plus hr. Bus or boat: 2-plus hr. (190km/118 miles). Theater:* ☎ *275/302-2009. Daily 8am–7:30pm; 8am–5pm winter. Site admission 6€. Buy theater tickets from 5pm on performance day. See p 122 for performance info.* ●

The
Savvy Traveler

Before You Go

Government Tourist Offices

In the U.S.: Greek National Tourism Organization (GNTO), Olympic Tower, 645 Fifth Ave., Ste. 903, New York, NY 10022 (☎ 212/421-5777; fax 212/826-6940; www.greek tourism.com). **In Canada:** Hellenic Tourism Organization, 1500 Don Mills Rd., Ste. 102, Toronto, Ontario M3B-3K4 (☎ 416/968-2220; fax 416/968-6533). **In the U.K. and Ireland:** GNTO, 4 Conduit St., London W1S 2DJ (☎ 020/7495-9300; fax 020/7495-4057; www.gnto.co.uk). **In Australia and New Zealand:** GNTO, 37–49 Pitt St., Sydney, New South Wales 2000 (☎ 02/9241-1663; fax 02/9241-2499). **In Greece:** GNTO, 7 Tsoha St., Ambelokipi, Athens 11521 (☎ 210/870-7000; www.gnto.gr); 26 Amalias Ave., Syntagma, Athens 10557 (☎ 210/331-0392; fax 210/331-0640; www.gnto.gr).

The Best Times to Go

Athens temperatures are most comfortable in the **fall** and full-bloom **spring,** when it is also at its most beautiful. It is hottest in June and July, but this is also the time when **summer** festivals are in full swing. The northern *Meltemia* (Etesian winds) blow from mid-July to mid-August, when chilly Aegean Sea water is warmest. Except for tourist areas like Plaka, this city of four million empties during the August 15 national holiday week, when most Greeks go on holiday. As the earth becomes desolate when Demeter is saddened by the loss of her daughter, Persephone, to the underworld each **winter,** most resorts too turn bleak and shut down, usually by October. Museums work on a reduced schedule that lasts until

April, and most hotels also go on a winter-long hiatus. Greece—and the budget hotels that remain open— can get very chilly from November to March.

Festivals & Special Events

SPRING   The Greek calendar revolves around religious holidays, and **Orthodox Easter** (*Pascha*), usually a week later than Western Easter, is the nation's biggest. Many fast during Holy Week. Church bells toll on Good Friday, and the parish walks a candlelit procession. On Saturday night, people go to their neighborhood church just before midnight with candles to celebrate Resurrection (*Anastasi*), when the priest brings out the holy flame brought from Jerusalem and passes it to the congregation, who light each other's candles while saying "*Christos anesti*" (Christ is risen). Youths light fireworks, and congregants return with their still-lit candles to bless their homes by "drawing" a cross on the door frame with the candle's smoke. The Lenten fast is broken by cracking red-dyed eggs and eating soup made with lamb innards. Lamb is spit-roasted on Sunday on rooftops, in garages, in backyards, and in parks. Easter Monday is a national holiday.

SUMMER   **Music, art, and film festivals** kick off in May and June (see p 122). Athens is barren in August, especially around August 15 (for the **Assumption of the Virgin** holiday).

FALL   The **International Trade Fair** (☎ 231/012-9111; www.tif.gr) in Thessaloniki dominates in September, while in Athens there is the **International Film Festival**

Previous page: The Metro passing under the illuminated Hephaisteion temple in the Ancient Agora.

ATHENS'S AVERAGE TEMPERATURES & PRECIPITATION						
	JAN	FEB	MAR	APR	MAY	JUNE
Temp (°F)	49	50	53	60	68	76
Temp (°C)	9	10	12	16	20	24
Rainfall (in.)	1.80	1.90	1.70	1.10	0.70	0.40
Rainfall (cm)	4.57	4.83	4.32	2.79	1.78	1.02
	JULY	AUG	SEPT	OCT	NOV	DEC
Temp (°F)	81	80	74	65	58	52
Temp (°C)	27	27	23	18	14	11
Rainfall (in.)	0.20	0.20	0.50	1.90	2.00	2.60
Rainfall (cm)	0.51	0.51	1.27	4.83	5.08	6.60

(www.aiff.gr). Fashionistas arrive for **Fashion Week** (www.hfda.gr) in October at Zappeion Gardens, and the original **Marathon** (☎ 210/933-1113; www.athensclassic marathon.gr), from Marathon to Athens, takes place in November.

WINTER Big hotels vie for the most exotic and scrumptious meal title, and city streets and squares are decked out in December and January for **Christmas** and **New Year's** festivities, with central Syntagma Square getting the biggest Christmas tree, a carousel, and lots of street stalls. New Year's is also celebrated there, or at Kotzia Square in front of City Hall. Men dive into frigid waters at the port of Piraeus to retrieve the cross on **Epiphany** (Jan 6). February's pre-Lent **Carnival** (*Karnavali* or *Apokries*) is celebrated nationwide with costume parades and merriment. People bop each other with plastic bats in Athens's Plaka neighborhood. When Lent begins on **Clean Monday** in February or March, Greeks traditionally go on a Lenten-food picnic and fly kites, especially on Filopappou Hill. Military parades are seen on **Independence Day,** March 25.

The Weather

Basically there are two seasons, borne out by the traditional weather-change send-offs "*Kalo Himona*" (Good Winter) or "*Kalo Kalokairi*"

(Good Summer). Summer, generally starting after Easter, is very hot and dry, sometimes reaching 40°C (104°F). As the saying goes, only mad dogs and Englishmen would venture out in the midday sun, hence the siesta between 3 and 6pm. The seasonal north (Etesian) winds run mid-July to mid-August, but it can get very windy anytime, stopping ferry transport. Torrential rains can also occur quickly.

Winter is mild and rainy with snowfalls not unheard of. It can also go from warm to downright numbing. Many buildings are not insulated, and the centrally controlled heating is often intermittent, making the cold season very long indeed.

Useful Websites

www.culture.gr: The culture ministry of Greece's Web page for museums and sites.

www.gnto.gr: The Greece tourism ministry's site.

www.ticketnet.gr: See what Arts & Entertainment events are in town.

www.hnms.gr: The Hellenic National Meteorological Service (weather).

www.oasa.gr: Public transportation site, including maps.

www.poseidon.ncmr.gr: The Hellenic Centre for Marine Research's weather site, including sea-surface temperature.

Cell (Mobile) Phones

As in all of Europe, **GSM (Global System for Mobiles)** phones work in Greece, but making and receiving calls while abroad can be pricey. It might be cheaper to buy one for use while in Athens. **Kapa Change,** at 52 Mitropoleos St. (☎ 210/331-0493; www.kapatravel.gr), sells mobiles from 25€ and a Greek phone number from 1€.

Getting **There**

By Plane

Eleftherios Venizelos, the Athens International Airport (☎ 210/353-0000; www.aia.gr) in Spata (27km/17 miles east of Athens), is a major south-European hub. There are two airport information desks at each end of the arrivals hall, three ATMs, two free Internet kiosks, a pharmacy, a post office, a money exchange machine manned at the departure level, and a few shops. The **Greek National Tourism Organization** (GNTO or EOT in Greek; ☎ 210/353-0445) is also in the arrivals hall, alongside private tour agencies that can book hotels.

Getting into Town from the Airport

The **Metro** subway (☎ 210/519-4012; www.ametro.gr) goes to central Athens (45 min.) from the airport, or you can take the suburban railway **Proastiakos** (☎ 210/527-2000; www.oasa.gr; www.proastiakos.gr) to Larissa Station, Athens's central railway station (40 min.), to the port of Piraeus (1 hr.), or to Corinth (1½ hr.). Tickets for either the Metro or Proastiakos are 6€ (3€ for children 17 and under or adults 65 and over; free for children 5 and under; 10€ for two people; 15€ for three people), which you validate or "cancel" in machines before you get to the shared platform. Don't forget—fines up to 60 times the fare are levied if you don't cancel and get caught. Metro and Proastiakos services run from about 7am to 11pm.

Public buses (☎ 185; www.oasa.gr) terminate outside the arrivals hall, and tickets, which you validate on machines on the bus, cost 3.20€. Both the X94 and X95 run to the Ethniki Amyna Metro station on Line Three if you want to take the rest of your journey into town on the Metro from there. X95 continues to central Syntagma Square, about a 70-minute trip. Bus X96 stops at the Faliro Metro station (which connects with the **tram**) before continuing on to the port of Piraeus Metro station; both of those stops are also on Metro Line One.

A **taxi** will cost around 30€, and around 40€ between midnight and 5am. Trip time is 30 minutes to an hour, depending on traffic. There are additional charges, such as for luggage, tolls, and time, which do not appear on the meter and therefore work in (too many) dishonest drivers' favor. The charges are usually listed on a card mounted on the dashboard, where the driver's ID should also be. Be guarded.

By Ferry

Boats from Ancona, Bari, Brindisi, and Venice, Italy arrive daily to the ports of Patras and Igoumenitsa. Trip times vary depending on the ferry you take and your departure and arrival points, but it takes from 10 to 17 hours to get to the main arrival port of Patras. Eurailpass holders should consult **www.raileurope.com** or their pass booklets

Italy to Greece

Getting to Athens from Italy by ferry can take 3 days (plus food, lodging, and transport costs); it may be cheaper to fly. Check **www.skyscanner.net** to e-book cheap flights from Milan or Venice; try **www.flyairone.it** from Rome, or check the **Rome airport** (☎ 06/65951; www.adr.it) for a dozen daily flights. Cheap flights in and out of Athens can also be found through **www.airtickets.gr**.

to see which operators will honor their passes. Note that you'll have to pay a port tax, fuel fees, and a seasonal surcharge (16€–26€) even if you do have a pass.

Trains from the port at Patras (☎ 1110 or 261/063-9102) to Athens take 3½ hours and cost 5.30€, while a long-distance **KTEL bus** (☎ 210/514-7310 in Athens; 261/062-3887 in Patras) that leaves every 30 to 45 minutes takes 2½ hours and costs about 15€.

By Cruise Ship
Cruise ship passengers can get from the port of Piraeus into Athens (10km/6 miles/20 min.) by taking bus no. 049 at the terminus on main Akti Miaouli Avenue, near the international passenger terminal, to the terminus on Athinas Street in Athens. You can also walk around the harbor (15–20 min.) to the Piraeus Metro station (20 min. to Athens) or hail a cab (15–30 min. to Athens; about 10€).

By Train
Greece is connected to the Balkans, Eastern Europe, Russia, and Turkey rather lurchingly by rail, with international trains terminating in the northern port city of Thessaloniki. Check the English page of the German website **Die Bahn** (http://reiseauskunft.bahn.de) for international journeys, and the **Hellenic National Railway** (OSE; ☎ 1110;

www.ose.gr) for domestic travel. You can reserve up to a month in advance, but you must buy your ticket at a domestic station or OSE-affiliated travel agency not less than 48 hours before your journey. The two OSE ticket offices in Athens are at 1 Karolou St. (☎ 1110), open Monday to Friday 8am to 3pm, and at 6 Sina St. (international travel: ☎ 210/362-7947; domestic travel: ☎ 1110; from abroad: ☎ 210/362-1039), open Monday to Saturday 8am to 3:30pm.

There are some 11 trains daily from Thessaloniki to Athens's relatively small Larissa OSE Station (☎ 210/529-8829), and the trip takes from 4½ to 8 hours for overnights, which have sleepers that range from 54€ in a single compartment to 24€ in a six-bed. Larissa Station has luggage storage, a restaurant, a platform cantina, and a train information counter. Only same-day tickets can be purchased in the building's main entrance. Advance tickets are available from the south end (outside the entrance) toward the kiosk.

By Bus
The KTEL regional **Bus Terminal A** (with buses to Patras, points north and south, Peloponnese, and western Greece) is at 100 Kifissou St. (☎ 210/512-4910). The local bus 051 from Menandrou Street, west of Omonia Square in Athens, gets you

there. **Bus Terminal B** (to central Greece, including Delphi and Meteora) is at 260 Liossion St. (☎ 210/831-7153), and is served by a dozen city buses that go to Attiki Metro station. The driver usually drops passengers off near Kato Patissia station on Line One, however, before reaching the terminal. Buses to sites in Attica (including Cape Sounion and Marathon) leave from

Aigyptou Square on Patission Street (☎ 210/822-5148, 210/880-8080; www.ktelattikis.gr), just past the National Archaeological Museum. Buses going abroad, to Turkey and Albania for example, are run by **KTEL** (☎ 1421; www.ktel. org), the **Hellenic National Railway** (see "By Train" above), and private travel agencies.

Getting **Around**

By Bus

Local buses and trolleys run from about 5am to 10pm, occasionally to midnight, depending on the line. Tickets are .80€ and are bought in advance from *periptera* (kiosks) or at bus-ticket booths at some bus stops. Families with four or more children are entitled to reduced fare. Tickets, which are good for all modes of public transport, are good for 90 minutes, and must be validated (or "canceled") in the machine upon boarding. **Athens Urban Transport Organization** (OASA; ☎ 185; www.oasa.gr) puts out a route map, and you can check it online. There is a state-run hop-on sightseeing bus that does a circuit of all the main sites in 80 to 90 minutes. The 5€ ticket can be purchased on the bus (no. 400), which is good for 24 hours on all public transport within the city.

By Metro

There are three lines, and tickets for the much older **green Line One** (run by ISAP), the **red Line Two,** and the **blue Line Three** are .80€, and you can use them to travel on all three lines and all modes of public transport for 90 minutes. The trains aren't color-coded—just the signage.

A 3€ ticket buys you 24 hours; a 10€ ticket gets you 7 days. These can be purchased at bus-ticket booths, kiosks, and tram, Metro, and Proastiakos stations. See the **Metro** (www.ametro.gr) and **OASA** (www. oasa.gr) websites for more options.

By Tram

The **tram** (www.tramsa.gr) goes from central Syntagma Square to the coast, where it branches west to the Neo Faliro district and nearby Peace and Friendship stadium, or southeast past beaches at Alimos and Hellenikon to Glyfada and Voula.

Tram tickets, purchased at station vending machines or at manned ticket booths at some stations, cost .80€ and are valid on all modes of public transport within 90 minutes of validation. The tram runs from 5am to midnight.

By Taxi

Taxis are yellow and cheap. The rate, normally posted on the dashboard, is 1€ to start, with a minimum charge of 2.80€. The meter rate of .34€ per kilometer nearly doubles if you leave the city limits (not including the airport) or for travel between midnight and 5am. Other small-change add-ons include going to the airport or pickup from a port or bus station, heavy luggage, tolls, and time. Round up, usually to the nearest euro.

Taxis rather "greenly" pick up other passengers going to destinations on the route, but each party pays separately. The driver tells you the charge, but you can check the meter amount when you get in and pay the difference when you get out, not forgetting the extra minimum or pickup charge. If you got in first and you don't want your driver to pick up other passengers, say so, but the practice helps keep the rates down.

Taxis can be difficult to find at times, especially around 3pm (the shift change) and 11:30pm (when they all wait till the night tariff kicks in). There are some 15 taxi companies in Athens that you can call to make an appointment with or for immediate service—and pay 2€ to 5€ extra for the privilege. Two are **Attika** (☎ 210/341-0553) and **Ikaros** (☎ 210/515-2800). Or call **Limotours,** 20 Syngrou Ave. (☎ 210/922-0333; www.limotours.gr); **Athens Luxury Transportation Services** (☎ 210/322-4587; www.athens exclusivetaxi.gr); or **George the Famous Taxi Driver** (☎ 210/963-7030; georgetaxitours@yahoo.com) for trips to the airport, tours, and so on.

By Car

Driving in central Athens is not recommended. Traffic is heavy, most streets are one-way or pedestrian, parking is difficult, drivers can be erratic, and the historic center is fairly compact. However, if you'd like to drive, there are many car-rental offices located at the top of Syngrou Avenue in Makriyanni. Or look for the best deal from an online "supermarket." Try **www.travelsupermarket. com** or **www.sidestep.com**.

By Foot

All the main sites in Athens are best seen on foot or in one or two short Metro stops. Much of the historic and commercial center is pedestrianized, including touristy Plaka, while a cobblestone walkway—the "Unification of the Archaeological Sites of Athens"—was completed in 2004 and links up the marble Panathenian Stadium, the Temple of Zeus, Syntagma Square, Hadrian's Arch, the Parthenon, Filopappou Hill, the Ancient Agora and Thissio, Monastiraki Square, the Roman Agora, and the ancient Kerameikos cemetery and Technopolis cultural center in Gazi.

Wear comfortable shoes and watch your step—a lot of sidewalks are blocked (by cars, motorcycles, or trees), slippery (paved with marble), soiled (Athenians like their beasts, stray or otherwise), or uneven (missing a paving stone or waterworks lid), not to mention plagued by the overhead menaces of air-conditioning drips and pigeon droppings. Furthermore, drivers rarely yield right of way to pedestrians, so don't blindly step into the road even if the little green man says to do so. Always look both ways before crossing the street, including on one-way streets and pedestrian roads.

Fast **Facts**

APARTMENT RENTALS   Check long-term rates of apartment hotels in the Lodging chapter, the classifieds in the weekly **Athens News** (www.athensnews.gr), or online sites such as **www.vacationhome rentals.com** or **http://athens. craigslist.gr**.

AREA CODES The country code for Greece is **30**. Domestically, 10 digits are needed, which includes the area code. Athens is 210 or 211 plus seven digits; Thessaloniki is 2310 plus six digits, as is Patras (2610) and other urban areas. A five-digit area code is used elsewhere in the country. Mobile (cell) phones do not follow the area-code rule but require 10 digits and begin with 6.

ATMS & CASH POINTS ATMs are widely available—Greece has a lot of banks—and most are open to the street. Check the international system your bank card belongs to (on your card and on ATMs) and make your withdrawal. Both your bank and the Greek bank will charge you for the transaction.

BABYSITTING Hotels usually indicate if they can arrange babysitting.

BANKING HOURS Generally, banks are open Monday to Thursday 8am to 2:30pm and Friday 8am to 2pm.

BIKE RENTALS For tours and rentals, try **Pame Volta** (☎ 210/675-2886; www.pamevolta.gr).

BUSINESS HOURS Work hours in Greece differ by season, day of the week, and type of business. Shops are generally open Monday, Wednesday, and Saturday from 8:30am to 2pm; Tuesday, Thursday, and Friday from 8:30am to 2pm and again from 5:30 to 8:30pm. Chain stores, supermarkets, and department stores remain open through the midday siesta Monday through Saturday. In tourist areas, stores are generally open longer, as well as on Sundays.

CONSULATES & EMBASSIES **U.S. Embassy:** 91 Vas. Sofias Ave. (☎ 210/721-2951; www.usembassy. gr); Metro: Megaron Mousikis. **Canadian Embassy:** 4 Ioannou Gennadiou St. (☎ 210/727-3400;

www.athens.gc.ca); Metro: Evangelismos. **U.K. Embassy:** 1 Ploutarchou St. (☎ 210/727-2600; www. british-embassy.gr); Metro: Evangelismos. **Australian Embassy:** Thon Building, Kifissias and Alexandras aves. (☎/fax 210/870-4000; www. greece.embassy.gov.au); Metro: Ambelokipi. **New Zealand Consulate:** 76 Kifissias Ave. (☎ 210/ 692-4136); Metro: Ambelokipi. **Irish Embassy:** 7 Vas. Konstantinou St., opposite Panathenian Stadium (☎ 210/732-2771).

CUSTOMS There is Customs control for extra-Schengen-originated (mainly non-European) flights.

DINING For breakfast and as a snack, countless holes-in-the-wall sell various pies, *tiropita* (cheese), *spanakopita* (spinach), and *bougatsa* (cream/semolina) being the most common. *Koulouri* (round bread "sticks") are sold in the street, as are roasted chestnuts and corn on the cob. The midday meal, eaten at around 2 or 3pm, is the biggest. Dinner hour is 10pm.

DOCTORS & DENTISTS See "Emergencies."

ELECTRICITY Electric current in Greece is 220 volts AC, alternating at 50 cycles. Appliances from North America that are not dual voltage will require a transformer and a round two-prong adapter plug.

EMERGENCIES For emergencies throughout Greece, dial ☎ **100** for police assistance or ☎ **171** for the Tourist Police. Dial ☎ **199** to report a fire and ☎ **166** for an ambulance. The EU-wide ☎ **112** is a multilingual service for all kinds of emergencies.

If you need an English-speaking doctor or dentist, call your embassy for advice or the 24-hour **SOS Doctors** (☎ 1016; www.sosiatroi.gr). Some American- and British-trained doctors and hospitals offering emergency services advertise in the English-language *Athens News*, available at kiosks that sell international press. Most of the larger hotels have doctors whom they can call for you in an emergency.

There is a walk-in **first-aid clinic** on the corner of Panagi Tsaldari and Socratous streets, near Omonia Square (1 block up from Geraniou St.). One private hospital is **Euroclinic** (☎ 210/641-6600; www.euro clinic.gr), at 9 Athanasiadou St. (off Soutsou St.); Metro: Ambelokipi.

EVENTS   The most complete listings for arts or entertainment are in Greek only. Try the weekly *Athinorama* or *TimeOut* and ask your hotel or at tourist information for assistance. There are limited listings in the weekly *Athens News* or daily *Kathimerini* section inside the *International Herald Tribune*. For festivals around the country, look up **www.greecetravel.com/holidays**. For happenings in Athens, see **www.dolphin-hellas.gr**, and click on Cultural Events.

FAMILY TRAVEL   Expect preferential treatment. Ask your hotel for special needs such as cots, bottle warming, and connecting rooms. Most restaurants welcome children, but check stroller access; same for museums and sites. Children 5 and under ride free on public transport; children 17 and under and seniors get 50% off the Metro and Proastiakos rail; families with four or more children are eligible for reduced fares on buses.

GAY & LESBIAN TRAVELERS   Check **www.gaygreece.gr** or **www.10 percent.gr**. The Gazi area has many gay-friendly bars and clubs.

HOLIDAYS   Greece celebrates New Year's Day (Jan 1); Epiphany (Jan 6); Clean (Ash) Monday (Feb or Mar); Independence Day (Mar 25); Good Friday and Easter Sunday and Monday (in the Orthodox calendar, Apr or May); Labor Day (May 1); Whit Monday (May or June); the Assumption of the Virgin (Aug 15); Ochi Day

(Oct 28); Christmas and the day after (Dec 25–26); and the student uprising commemoration march to the U.S. Embassy (Nov 17).

INSURANCE   Check if you're covered already from medical, home, work, or travel policies in your home country. You can try for the best deal through "supermarket" websites such as **www.moneysupermarket. com/travelinsurance**. EU residents are covered with the **European Health Insurance Card** (EHIC; www.ehic.org.uk).

INTERNET ACCESS   Most hotels provide Internet access, and there are many Internet cafes around town (see p 123).

LOST & FOUND   File a report at the nearest police station. On trains call ☎ **1110;** on the Metro call ☎ **210/ 327-9630** or go to Syntagma station.

MAIL & POSTAGE   Overseas postcard stamps cost .67€ and are available at many kiosks and shops selling postcards. The main post office is at Syntagma Square at Mitropoleos Street; another is at 100 Aeolou Street, just southeast of Omonia Square. The parcel post office is at 60 Mitropoleos St. Hours are Monday to Friday 7:30am to 8pm. The Aeolou and Syntagma branches are also open Saturday 7:30am to 2pm, and Syntagma is also open on Sunday 9am to 1:30pm. Regular post offices are open Monday to Friday 7:30am to 2pm.

MONEY   Greece's currency is the euro. In this cash society, most non-chain stores and restaurants do not accept credit or debit cards; try to have bills in small denominations. Apart from ATM withdrawals, you can get money wired through **Money Gram** agents (www.money gram.com) and **Western Union** (☎ 801/113-8000), which are located at post offices and exchange bureaus, such as at Syntagma Square and at 52 Mitropoleos St.

There's an **American Express** bank at 43 Akademias St. (☎ 210/363-5960).

NEWSPAPERS & MAGAZINES English-language newspapers are found at foreign-press newsstands, including all the kiosks at the top of Ermou Street at Syntagma Square. The *Athens News* (www.athensnews. gr) is a weekly English-language newspaper, and *Kathimerini* (www.ekathimerini.com) is a daily found inside the *International Herald Tribune*. A foreign-press kiosk at Omonia Square is open 24 hours (see p 73).

PARKING Parking is difficult and almost always bumper-to-bumper parallel. You can take your chances and park on streets where you see other cars (the signs are confusing), see if your hotel has free parking, or go to a pay parking lot. Charges are about 5€ for the first hour and 16€ a day.

PASSES A 12€ ticket to the **Acropolis**—a coupon booklet—is valid for 4 days, and includes admission coupons to the Acropolis, Ancient Agora, Theater of Dionysos and south slope, Tower of the Winds, Kerameikos Cemetery, Roman Forum, north slope, and the Temple of Olympian Zeus.

The **New Acropolis Museum** will open at the end of 2008 or early 2009. Many categories, including archaeology students, are admitted free (ask, or check www.culture.gr). **Eurailpass** holders should check their booklets for discounts on hotels, tours, and domestic ferry journeys.

PASSPORTS Most foreigners, including North Americans who stay less than 3 months, do not need a visa, just a valid passport. A passport usually is required when registering in a hotel and kept until checkout.

PHARMACIES Pharmacies are marked by green and sometimes red crosses, and are usually open from 8 or 10am to 2pm and again from 5 to 8:30pm on Tuesday, Thursday, and Friday. After-hours locations are posted (in Greek) in pharmacy windows, found by dialing ☎ 1434 (in Greek), or by looking in an *Athens News* or *Kathimerini* newspaper or on www.ekathimerini.com. You can get antibiotics and other over-the-counter meds without a prescription, and advice for simple ailments.

POLICE Dial ☎ 100. For help dealing with a troublesome taxi driver or hotel, restaurant, or shop owner, call the **Tourist Police** at ☎ 171; they're on call 24 hours and speak English, as well as other foreign languages.

SAFETY Apart from averting a fall on an uneven sidewalk and giving selfish drivers the right of way, visitors have only a few minor concerns. Young women may get propositioned by shopkeepers in tourist areas and the unsuspecting may be scammed but not harmed. Greece has a low crime rate and you can safely walk the streets well into the night, but pick-pocketing, mostly on public transport during busy times, is a problem. Motorcycle thieves may also target the vulnerable by pulling up alongside and grabbing shoulder bags, pulling people over in the process.

Major hospitals rotate emergency duty daily; call ☎ 1434 to hear recorded information in Greek on whose turn it is, or ☎ 112 for the multilingual European Union emergency hotline, or consult the English edition of the *Kathimerini* daily newspaper, distributed with the *International Herald Tribune*, sold wherever you see the foreign press and online at www.ekathimerini.com.

SENIOR TRAVELERS Seniors (60 or 65 and over) pay less at most museums and sites, on the Metro and Proastiakos suburban railway (65 and over), and at organized beaches (65 and over). Always ask if discounts are available. **Elderhostel** (www.elderhostel.org) does tours. For accessibility issues, see "Travelers with Disabilities," below.

SMOKING Smoking is allowed almost anywhere, but may raise an eyebrow in hospital waiting rooms.

STAYING HEALTHY Sunglasses and sunscreen are needed in summer, and a hat helps. Keep in the shade as much as possible, and keep water with you, which is widely available in corner stores, kiosks, sandwich shops, and the like. Embassies can provide info on English-speaking doctors if you fall ill. State hospitals treat minor emergencies free of charge; otherwise, admission is possible through a doctor.

TAXES A value-added tax (VAT), normally 19%, is included in the price of goods, less for items like books and food. Keep your receipts and go to **Eurochange** in the airport's departure hall.

TELEPHONES Most public phones accept only phone cards, which are available at kiosks. **Telecards** come in denominations from 3€ to 18€. Local calls cost .03€ per minute. International rates vary, with calls to the U.S., Canada, and Australia (Zone I) costing .29€ per minute. **Prepaid calling cards** are available at kiosks, post offices, OTEshop (phone company) outlets, and money-exchange bureaus (which can also tell you what card gives the best rate for the country you want to call). Denominations are usually 5€, 10€, and 20€. Other phone companies include **AT&T** (☎ 00/800-1311); **MCI** (☎ 00/800-1211); and **Sprint** (☎ 00/800-1411). For international phone assistance, dial ☎ **139.**

TIPPING Round up to the nearest euro in a taxi; leave 10% to 20% at restaurants and bars. Restaurants include a service charge in the bill, but many add a 10% tip. Hotel chambermaids should get at least 1€ per day and bellhops 1€ to 2€ depending on the service.

TOILETS Metro stations do not have toilets, but some have coin-operated ones nearby. Some squares have public toilets, but most people use the facilities at restaurants and cafes.

TOURIST OFFICES The **Greek National Tourism Organization (GNTO)** head office is at 7 Tsochas St. (☎ 210/870-7000; www.gnto.gr); the central information desk is at 26 Amalias St. (☎ 210/331-0392).

Two good online resources are the privately maintained **www.greecetravel.com** and, for sites of interest, the Hellenic Ministry of Culture's **www.culture.gr**.

The **Tourist Police,** 43 Veikou St. (☎ 171 or 210/920-0724), south of the Acropolis, offer round-the-clock tourist information in English.

TOURIST TRAPS & SCAMS Walk against the traffic to avoid motorcycle-riding purse snatchers. Don't accept offers of possibly drugged food or water from strangers at tourist sites, and avoid touts that take lone males to hostess bars, or fast friends who promise hotel-room parties. You will pay exorbitant bills if you succumb. Taxi drivers are notorious for overcharging, or giving you change for a smaller denomination bill. Put your hand over the keypad at ATMs when you enter your PIN to avoid card theft.

TRAVELERS WITH DISABILITIES Athens's accessibility consciousness is fledgling. The **European Network for Accessible Tourism** (☎ 210/614-8380; www.accessibletourism.org) has information, or check the relevant transport and hotel websites for accessibility. See **www.europeforall.com** or **www.sath.org** for further information on accessible travel in Greece. The **Tactile Museum for the Blind,** by appointment only, is at 198 Doiranis St. (☎ 210/941-5222).

Athens: **A Brief History**

4500–4000 B.C. The area around Acropolis hill is first settled.

1300–1200 B.C. Mycenaean palace remains found atop Acropolis in Athinai, a cultural, administrative, and military center.

510 B.C. Spartans invade Athens.

508–507 B.C. First Athenian democracy established.

490–480 B.C. Persians defeated at battle of Marathon; fleet defeated at Salamis.

478 B.C. Athens League rule over Greek cities formed.

447–438 B.C. Parthenon built during "Golden Age of Greece."

322 B.C. Macedonian occupation of Athens.

58 B.C. Athens under Roman domination.

A.D. 50 Apostle Paul preaches at Areopagus.

267 Black Sea region Heruls (Goths) raze Athens.

4th–5th C. Athens a major philosophical and education center; Hadrian's Library rebuilt.

529 Justinian I closes the Academy.

582 Slavs and Avars sack the city.

12th–15th C. Athens conquered by Franks, Catalans, Venetians, and Ottomans.

1687–1688 Venetian bomb hits Parthenon; Venetian rule.

17th–18th C. Ottoman rule.

1801–1803 Britain's Lord Elgin removes metope sculptures from the Parthenon and ships them to England; widespread pillaging of antiquities, especially by England and France.

1821–1830 Greek War of Independence.

1834 Capital moved from Nafplion to Athens.

1843 Constitution demanded from installed Bavarian King Otto in front of the palace, now Parliament, at Syntagma (Constitution) Square.

1896 First modern Olympic Games.

1922–1923 Greece receives 1.1 million refugees from Asia Minor (Turkey); Athens's population doubles between 1920 and 1928.

1940–1941 Italy and then Germany invade and occupy Greece in World War II.

1944 Churchill and Stalin agree on respective spheres of influence over Greece and Romania.

1946–1949 Cold War hostilities fuel civil war.

1956 First general election in which women vote.

1967 Junior disgruntled officers, "the colonels," proclaim martial law, auguring in a brutal 7-year dictatorship.

Nov 17, 1973 Tanks invade Polytechnic campus during student protests; at least 34 killed.

1974 Junta collapses after failed coup in Cyprus; Turkey invades the island. Monarchy abolished in referendum.

1981 Greece becomes 10th member of EEC (European Economic Community).

1991 Greece clashes with newly independent Former Yugoslav Republic of Macedonia (FYROM) over name.

Jan 1996 Greece and Turkey come to brink of war over islet of Imia.

1999 Relations thaw with mutual assistance after earthquakes strike Turkey and Greece.

Feb 3–5, 2000 Turkish Foreign Minister Ismail Cem makes first official visit in 40 years.

Sept 2000 *Express Samina* sinks near Paros killing 80, the worst ferry disaster in 35 years.

May 4–5, 2001 Pope John Paul II visit a first to this Christian Orthodox country by a Roman pontiff since 1054; first ever to Athens.

2002 Greece enters Eurozone.

2004 Greece soccer team wins European Championship; Olympic Games held in Athens.

Athenian **Architecture**

Athens has been continuously inhabited for some 7,000 years, but not always as a capital city. Apart from ancient ruins staking space alongside apartment blocks, there are Byzantine churches, 19th-century neoclassical buildings and parks, and a 21st-century cobblestone walkway on which to view them all.

Aegean Bronze Age (2800–1100 B.C.)

The Mideast concept of a building as a work of art can be seen in Mycenaean palaces, which featured colorful frescoes contrasted with massive stone blocks. One was on the Acropolis, though no remains are left. For an idea of the style, Mycenaean artifacts are installed at the **National Archaeological Museum**.

Hellenic Age (8th–5th C. B.C.)

All the principle temples and monuments of Athens were built in this period in the much-celebrated Doric order: Rectangular temples were made of limestone, tufa, and marble, with tapered columns and unadorned capitals. Beautiful, strong Mount Pendeli marble (called Pentelic marble) was used on the 447–438 B.C. **Parthenon**, a perfection of the style.

Doric columns of Pentelic marble supporting the Parthenon.

Late 5th C. B.C.

Doric elements are combined with a more restrained version of the east Aegean's Ionic order, recognized by their volute (spiral-shape) capitals. This can be seen in the **Erechtheion** and the **Temple of Athena Nike** on the Acropolis.

5th C. B.C.–2nd C. A.D.

Corinthian-order acanthus capitals are evident in this time. These columns feature a leaf design, such as on the **Temple of Olympian Zeus**.

Volute capitals fronting the Erechtheion.

Early Christian Period (4th–7th C.)

Following Theodosius's ban of ancient cults in 437, Christianity exploded in Athens. The Christians did not build temples to the scale of ancient Greek monuments, rather constructing either cross-shaped domed churches or basilicas with sculpted capitals, cornices, and a screen separating the *naos* (church proper) from the sanctuary. Few basilicas have survived, but there is a small-scale reconstruction of one at the **Byzantine and Christian Museum**.

Byzantine Period (9th–15th C.)

A great number of churches from the Byzantine period have survived in Athens.

Typically, these are small, narrowly proportioned, domed, cross-shaped churches with inner frescoes and fine outer tile, brick masonry, and motifs, such as the **Kapnikarea.**

Post-Byzantine Period (16th–19th C.)

Architecture from this time is difficult to date, due to fragmentary remains of Frankish, Venetian, and Turkish monuments, which were constructed with a combination of older preexisting materials. For example, the **Daphni monastery,** originally constructed in the 6th century, underwent many changes after Byzantine rule: Gothic pointed arches, for example, were added by Catholic monks.

Neoclassical Period (19th–20th C.)

Athens was an idyllic city of 200,000 and was distinguished at the turn of the 19th century by a renewed interest in neoclassicism—a sentimental attachment to the indigenous ancient Greek traditions. Homes, courtyard gardens, and beautiful public buildings erected by wealthy Diaspora patrons all adhered to this style, epitomized by the **Academy of**

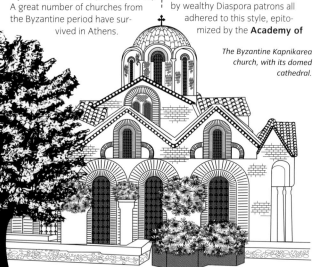

The Byzantine Kapnikarea church, with its domed cathedral.

The neoclassical Academy of Athens, which emulates the Ionic Erechtheion.

Athens, the **University of Athens,** and the **National Library,** all designed by the Hansen brothers. The 20th century marked a shift, though: The population reached 500,000 and new, modern multistoried office and apartment buildings went up, as was the fashion in other west European capitals. Greece was taking a cue from its installed German monarchy.

Interwar Period (1920s–1930s)

Athens grew to over one million inhabitants in the 1930s, due to the relocation of Asia Minor refugees in 1919 to 1922 and migration from the countryside, so the state turned a blind eye to illegal construction for much-needed housing. At the same time, British villas and garden suburbs in the north (in the **Psychiko** and **Filothei** neighborhoods) and south (in **Paleo Faliro**) sprouted up.

Postwar Period (20th C.)

With more rural migration the population continued to explode, and neighborhoods changed as property was sold to developers in exchange for one or more apartments in the building. An urban renewal project based on a 170-year-old plan to reclaim the chaotically overdeveloped and polluted city began in the 1990s, and the historic center was largely transformed to a pedestrian zone under the **Unification of the Archaeological Sites of Athens** plan, with restored and listed buildings and a pedestrian walkway connecting ancient sites.

Useful **Phrases & Menu Terms**

ENGLISH	GREEK	PRONUNCIATION
Hello/goodbye	Γειά σου/ Γειά σας	*Ya*-soo (singular, informal)/ *Ya*-sas (plural, singular polite)
Good morning	Καλημέρα	Ka-li-*me*-ra
Good afternoon/ evening	Καλησπέρα	Ka-li-*spe*-ra
Goodnight (night)	Καληνύχτα	Ka-li-*nich*-ta (*nik*-ta)
Yes	Ναι	Nai
No	Οχι	*O*-hi

162

ENGLISH	GREEK	PRONUNCIATION
Please/you're welcome	Παρακαλώ	Pa-ra-ka-*lo*
Thank you (very much)	Ευχαριστώ (πολή)	Ef-ha-ri-*stow* (po-*lee*)
How are you?	Τι κάνετε;	Ti *ka*-ne-te?
Fine, thank you	Μιά χαρά, ευχαριστώ	*Mya* ha-*ra*, ef-ha-ri-*stow*
Excuse me	Συγνώμη	Sig-*no*-mi
Sorry	Σόρι	*So*-ry
Give me . . .	Μου δώστε . . .	Mou *dhos*-te . . .
Do you speak English?	Μιλάτε αγγλικά;	Mi-*la*-te Angli-*ka*?
I understand	Καταλαβαίνω	Ka-ta-la-*ve*-no
I don't understand	Δεν καταλαβαίνω	Dhen ka-ta-la-*ve*-no
I know (it)	Το ξέρο	To *gze*-ro
Where is . . .	Που είναι . . .	Pou *ee*-ne . . .
the station	Ο σταθμός	o stath-*mos*
a post office	Το ταχιδρομίο	to ta-chi-dhro-*mee*-o
a bank	Η τράπεζα	ee *tra*-pe-za
a hotel	Το ξενοδοχέιω	to xe-no-dho-*hee*-o
a restaurant	Το εστιατόριο	to estia-*tow*-ree-o
a pharmacy/chemist	Το φαρμακέιο	to farma-*kee*-o
the toilet	Η τουαλέτα	ee tooa-*le*-ta
a hospital	Το νοσοκομέιο	to no-so-ko-*mee*-o
Left	Αριστερά	A-ri-ste-*ra*
Right	Δεξιά	Dhex-*ya*
Straight	Ευθύα	Ef-*thee*-a
Tickets	Εισιτήρια	Ee-see-*tee*-ria
How much does it cost?	Πόσο κάνει;	*Po*-so *ka*-ni?
A one-way ticket	Ενα απλό εισιτήριο	*E*-na ap-*lo* is-i-*ti*-rio
A round-trip ticket	Ενα εισιτήριο με επιστροφη	*E*-na is-i-*ti*-rio me e-pi-*stro*-fi
Is there a discount for . . .	Ηπάρχει έκπτωσι γία . . .	Ee-*par*-hi *ek*-pto-si yia . . .
family	Οικογένεια	ee-ko-*gen*-ya
children	Παιδιά	pe-*dhia*
students	Φοιτητές	fee-tee-*tes*
seniors	συνταξιούχος	syn-da-xi-*ou*-hos
What time is it?	Τη ώρα είναι;	Ti *o*-ra *ee*-ne?
When?	Πότε;	*Po*-teh?
When does (it) leave?	Πότε φεύγει;	*Po*-teh *fev*-gi?
This	Αυτό	Af-*tow*
Here	Εδώ	Eh-*dho*
There	Εκεί	Eh-*key*

Numbers

One (1)	Ενα	*E*-na
Two (2)	Δύο	*Dhee*-o
Three (3)	Τρία	*Tree*-a
Four (4)	Τέσσερα	*Te*-se-ra

ENGLISH	GREEK	PRONUNCIATION
Five (5)	Πέντε	*Pen*-de
Six (6)	Έξι	*E*-xi
Seven (7)	Επτά	Ep-*ta*
Eight (8)	Οκτό	Ok-*to*
Nine (9)	Εννιά	En-*ya*
Ten (10)	Δέκα	*Dhe*-ka
Eleven (11)	Έντεκα	*En*-dhe-ka
Twelve (12)	Δώδεκα	*Tho*-dhe-ka
Thirteen (13)	Δεκατρία	Dhe-ka-*tree*-a
Fourteen (14)	Δεκατέσσερα	Dhe-ka-*te*-se-da
Fifteen (15)	Δεκαπέντε	Dhe-ka-*pen*-de
Sixteen (16)	Δεκα-έξι	Dhe-ka-*eh*-xi
Seventeen (17)	Δεκα-επτά	Dhe-ka ep-*ta*
Eighteen (18)	Δεκα-οχτώ	Dhe-ka ok-*to*
Nineteen (19)	Δεκα-εννιά	Dhe-ka en-*ya*
Twenty (20)	Εικοσι	*Ee*-ko-see
Thirty (30)	Τριάντα	Tri-*an*-da
Forty (40)	Σαράντα	Sa-*ran*-da
Fifty (50)	Πενήντα	Pe-*nin*-da
One hundred (100)	Εκατό	Eh-ka-*to*

Menu Terms

Food	Φαγητό	Fa-gee-*to*
Water	Νερό	Neh-*ro*
Coffee	Καφέ	Ca-*feh*
Tea	Τσάι	*Tsa*-ee
A kilo/half-kilo of red/white wine	Ενα κιλό/Μισό κιλό κόκκινο/άσπρο κρασί	Ena kee-*lo*/mi-so kee-*lo* kok-kino/as-pro kra-*see*
The bill please	Το λογαριασμό παρακαλώ	To lo-ga-ri-az-*mo* pa-ra-ka-*lo*

* Roll the r's so they sound like a soft d. Dh sounds like the.

Useful **Toll-Free Numbers & Websites**

MAJOR INTERNATIONAL AIRLINES

AIR FRANCE
☎ *800/237-2747 (in U.S.)*
☎ *800/375-8723 (U.S. and Canada)*
☎ *087/0142-4343 (in U.K.)*
www.airfrance.com

ALITALIA
☎ *800/223-5730 (in U.S.)*
☎ *800/361-8336 (in Canada)*
☎ *087/0608-6003 (in U.K.)*
www.alitalia.com

BRITISH AIRWAYS
☎ *800/247-9297 (in U.S. and Canada)*
☎ *087/0850-9850 (in U.K.)*
www.british-airways.com

CHINA AIRLINES
☎ *800/227-5118 (in U.S.)*
☎ *022/715-1212 (in Taiwan)*
www.china-airlines.com

CONTINENTAL AIRLINES
☎ *800/523-3273 (in U.S. or Canada)*
☎ *084/5607-6760 (in U.K.)*
www.continental.com

DELTA AIR LINES
☎ 800/221-1212 (in U.S. or Canada)
☎ 084/5600-0950 (in U.K.)
www.delta.com

EGYPTAIR
☎ 212/581-5600 (in U.S.)
☎ 020/7734-2343 (in U.K.)
☎ 09/007-0000 (in Egypt)
www.egyptair.com

EL AL AIRLINES
☎ 972/3977-1111 (outside Israel)
☎ *2250 (from any phone in Israel)
www.elal.co.il

EMIRATES AIRLINES
☎ 800/777-3999 (in U.S.)
☎ 087/0243-2222 (in U.K.)
www.emirates.com

IBERIA AIRLINES
☎ 800/722-4642 (in U.S. and Canada)
☎ 087/0609-0500 (in U.K.)
www.iberia.com

LUFTHANSA
☎ 800/399-5838 (in U.S.)
☎ 800/563-5954 (in Canada)
☎ 087/0837-7747 (in U.K.)
www.lufthansa.com

OLYMPIC AIRLINES
☎ 800/223-1226 (in U.S.)
☎ 514/878-9691 (in Canada)
☎ 087/0606-0460 (in U.K.)
www.olympicairlines.com

SWISS AIR
☎ 877/359-7947 (in U.S. and Canada)
☎ 084/5601-0956 (in U.K.)
www.swiss.com

TURKISH AIRLINES
☎ 90/212444-0-849
www.thy.com

US AIRWAYS
☎ 800/428-4322 (in U.S. and Canada)
☎ 084/5600-3300 (in U.K.)
www.usairways.com

BUDGET AIRLINES

AEGEAN AIRLINES
☎ 210/626-1000 (in U.S., Canada, and U.K.)
www.aegeanair.com

AIR BERLIN
☎ 087/1500-0737 (in U.K.)
☎ 018/0573-7800 (in Germany)
☎ 180/573-7800 (all others)
www.airberlin.com

EASYJET
☎ 870/600-0000 (in U.S.)
☎ 090/5560-7777 (in U.K.)
www.easyjet.com

CAR-RENTAL AGENCIES

AUTO EUROPE
☎ 888/223-5555 (in U.S. and Canada)
☎ 0800/2235-5555 (in U.K.)
www.autoeurope.com

AVIS
☎ 800/331-1212 (in U.S. and Canada)
☎ 084/4581-8181 (in U.K.)
www.avis.com

BUDGET
☎ 800/527-0700 (in U.S.)
☎ 087/0156-5656 (in U.K.)
☎ 800/268-8900 (in Canada)
www.budget.com

DOLLAR
☎ 800/800-4000 (in U.S.)
☎ 800/848-8268 (in Canada)
☎ 080/8234-7524 (in U.K.)
www.dollar.com

HERTZ
☎ 800/645-3131
☎ 800/654-3001 (for international reservations)
www.hertz.com

THRIFTY
☎ 800/367-2277
☎ 918/669-2168 (international)
www.thrifty.com

MAJOR HOTEL CHAINS

BEST WESTERN INTERNATIONAL
☎ 800/780-7234 (in U.S. and Canada)
☎ 0800/393-130 (in U.K.)
www.bestwestern.com

DOUBLETREE HOTELS
☎ 800/222-TREE (800/222-8733) (in U.S. and Canada)
☎ 087/0590-9090 (in U.K.)
www.doubletree.com

HILTON HOTELS
☎ 800/HILTONS (800/445-8667) (in U.S. and Canada)
☎ 087/0590-9090 (in U.K.)
www.hilton.com

HOLIDAY INN
☎ 800/315-2621 (in U.S. and Canada)
☎ 0800/405-060 (in U.K.)
www.holidayinn.com

INTERCONTINENTAL HOTELS & RESORTS
☎ *800/424-6835 (in U.S. and Canada)*
☎ *0800/1800-1800 (in U.K.)*
www.ichotelsgroup.com

MARRIOTT
☎ *877/236-2427 (in U.S. and Canada)*
☎ *0800/221-222 (in U.K.)*
www.marriott.com

SHERATON HOTELS & RESORTS
☎ *800/325-3535 (in U.S.)*
☎ *800/543-4300 (in Canada)*
☎ *0800/3253-5353 (in U.K.)*
www.starwoodhotels.com/sheraton

WESTIN HOTELS & RESORTS
☎ *800-937-8461 (in U.S. and Canada)*
☎ *0800/3259-5959 (in U.K.)*
www.starwoodhotels.com/westin

Index

See also Accommodations and Restaurant indexes, below.

Photo **Credits**